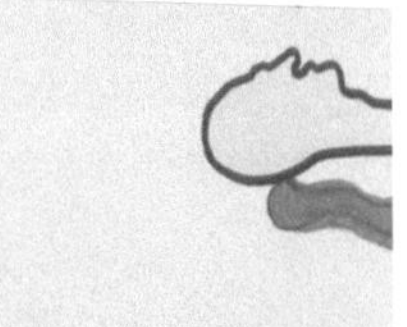

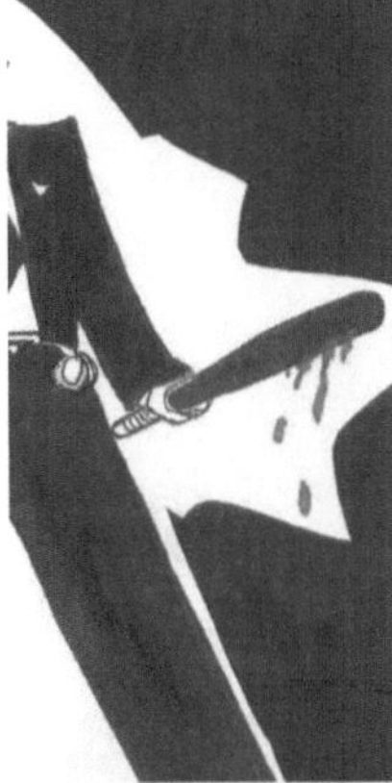

GOOD COP/ BAD COP

AN ANTHOLOGY
EDITED BY

EDWARD VIDAURRE & VINCENT COOPER

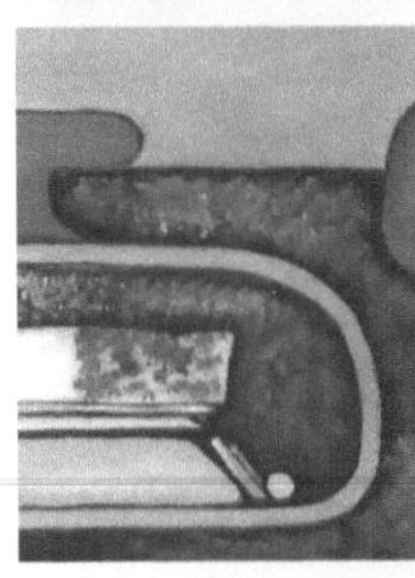

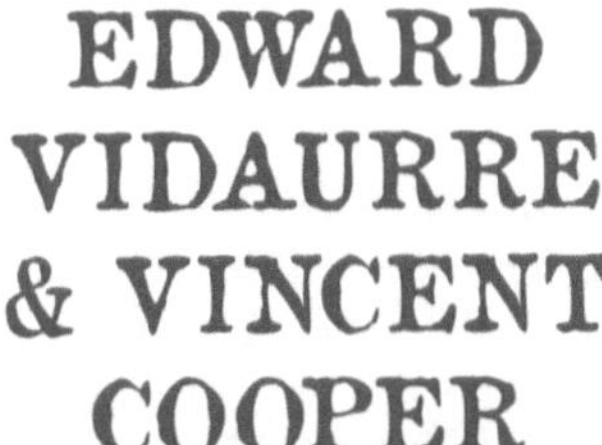

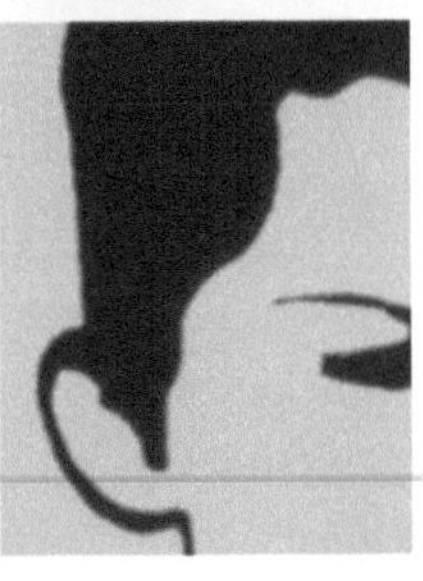

FlowerSong Press

Copyright © 2021 FlowerSong Press

ISBN: 978-1-953447-78-4

Library of Congress Number: 2021935982

Published by FlowerSong Press

in the United States of America.

www.flowersongpress.com

Set in Adobe Garamond Pro

Typeset and design by Matthew Revert

www.matthewrevert.com

Contents

Dear Reader,

You will find writings from authors ranging from not only the U.S.A. but from Canada, Mexico, Central America, Asia, Africa, and many other parts of the world. The violence against the community and its citizens is similar throughout the world, many times ending in incarceration, disability in many forms, or death with little to no justice. I grew up with beat cops. They walked the streets and were approachable, they handed out baseball cards and told us to not take drugs.

Then they started roughing us up for standing in our own neighborhoods. They called us names and asked if we wanted to go to jail. So, we started seeing them as a threat to our safety. We joined gangs and if we didn't we belonged by association. Cops became the boogeyman.

We still treated them with respect and feared making the wrong moves. They knew how we felt. Sometimes they placed drugs in our pockets or planted guns from crimes on our person. This book is a voice for our innocent men and women doing time in the world's penitentiaries.

This book is for those that witness violence. This book is for those that at one time wanted to be a police officer, you can still be one, you can be a good one. Not all cops are bad. But many are complicit and make them an enemy to justice.

We give love to officers like Eugene Goodman from the US Capitol, SP Celestina Kalu of Nigeria, and all those out there that truly live the oath every time they put on the badge. I'm sure there are many.

To the bad cop, find your true calling. Find your happiness, murder
and violence towards your citizens is not it. Seek help!

Still Breathing,

Edward Vidaurre
Editor-in-chief, FlowerSong Press

Dedicated to all the victims of police brutality, living and deceased

"They have the ability to take a person's freedom from them. On certain situations, they have the ability to take a person's reputation. And under certain circumstances, they have the authority to take a person's life."

—Daryl Gates, Chief of the Los Angeles Police Department (1978 to 1992)

"When you have police officers who abuse citizens, you erode public confidence in law enforcement. That makes the job of good police officers unsafe"

—Mary Frances Berry

VINCENT COOPER

Retrospect

4th grade Teacher, 1989
What do you want to be when you grow up Coop?
I don't know.
Come on. Do you want to be a Fireman? Police officer?
Can I tell the weather like Dallas Raines?
The meteorologist on TV?
Yes, I want to grow up and have cool hair and toss it around while telling everyone what the weather is.

Co-Worker, 2000
A Marine? You hate the government and George Bush. Why would you choose to protect him?
To be a fucking robot? You're crazy.

12-year-old daughter, 2015
Dad, can I have all your Marine uniforms?
You can have my cammies. They don't fit anymore.

Retrospect, 2020
I shoulda been a Chicano weatherman in southern California.

TEZOZOMOC

The Violent Guilt and Shame

"We are the survivors. We are the evidence of their crimes. They
don't want us as a reminder of what they did." -- John Trudell

And now it is winter in America.
It is the summer of our discontent.
The American colonial project
Clouds the view of our past.

In naturalizing nature
we take the right to life,
the sovereign liberty,
and we take the property;
and diminish its power.

These people
they are so naive
so free with their property.
If you ask them
they gladly share it with you.
> *"They would make fine servants…*
> *With fifty men we could subjugate*
> *Them all and make them do whatever*
> *We want." -- Christopher Columbus*

You see, it's, not satisfied
with merely holding people
in its grips
but wants to empty their brains

of form and content.
In cynicism, it turns to the past
of the oppressed people,
and distorts,
disfigures
and destroys.

As if Fredrick handed
Fanon his words…
The people must realize
power gives nothing
away for nothing.

The system works
Because it doesn't work.
It is a system of exploitation;
in its brutal form
which comes with guns
and re-inscription
of territory with its
cadastral maps
and its 11th century
juridical appropriations.
It occurs in subtle ways
a loan, food aid, black mail;
rendering a few to dictate
over the masses in the
name of civilization.

Today we can't see
the obfuscated

facade of neo-isms.
It was easy to see
the "Whites only,
No dogs or Mexicans" signs.

> *"Southern trees bear strange fruit,*
> *Blood on the leaves and blood at the root,*
> *Black bodies swinging in the southern breeze,*
> *Strange fruit hanging from the poplar trees.*
>
> *Pastoral scene of the gallant south,*
> *The bulging eyes and the twisted mouth,*
> *Scent of magnolias, sweet and fresh,*
> *Then the sudden smell of burning flesh.*
>
> *Here is the fruit for the crows to pluck,*
> *For the rain to gather, for the wind to suck,*
> *For the sun to rot, for the trees to drop,*
> *Here is a strange and bitter crop."— Abel Meeropol*

Today as survivors
we are constantly met
with our oppressors
explosive outbursts of anger,
their hypervigilance,
and their intense
sense of alienation.

The theft of the land
as eidetic dreams
are re-experienced

as a historical collective
traumatization;
re-inscribed on
the body without organs
or organs without bodies.

The eidetic dream of
role reversal.
That the marginal
people of color
will inflict the same on the
Deed holder.

The Americana of double speak;
the motif of split self;
the territorial telluric killer
and the righteous narrator
of western civilization.

The perpetrator trauma
is uncheck left only
with more violence.

No collective desensitization
or reprocessing. No
time perspective therapy.

The perpetrator trauma
of historical genocides
have not delivered
on the economic

cultural, psychological
reparations promised
by atonement and forgiveness.

Today when we make claims
to authenticity,
to culture,
to language,
to property,
to power;
we are met with
renewed acts of violence.

Outbursts of anger
engendering domestic violence
and street crime
against our claims as first peoples;
first nations,
first stewards
of the land and
the people.

We are met with
the collective emotional numbness of,
"Jews will not replace us!"

The estrangement
and apathetic violence of,
"Grab them by the pussy."

    "When asked by an anthropologist

what the Indians called America
before the white man came,
an Indian said simply, 'Ours.'"" —Vine Deloria Jr.

TEZOZOMOC

Wind Across My Window

Wind across my window
Michael Brown and the sirens outside
6 shells fly across my window
Wind across my window

Wind across my window
Slammed to the ground, Tanisha Anderson,
Took a knee to the back.
Wind across my window

Wind across my window
Terence Crutcher in Tulsa, OK
Betty Shelby and the bump-stock bullet
Of her whiteness as his hands were up.
Wind across my window.

Wind across my window
CD cases flying in the air
3 bullets, down went Alton Sterling
3 more in the back when he sat up.
Wind across my window.

Wind across my window
Walter Scott and 5 bullets in the back
And the simulacra of a taser
Wind across my window.

Wind across my window
Eric Harris and the mistaken
0.38 for a taser
Wind across my window

Wind across my window
Closed to his
House; rammed through
And a bullet through Tony Robinson's head.
Wind across my window.

Wind across my window
Rumain Brisbon's pill bottle
rolled on the floor
As the shots took him down.
Wind across my window.

Wind across my window
I had to shoot him;
12 year old with a BB gun;
Such was Tamir Rice's fate.
Wind across my window.

Wind across my window.
Laquan McDonald ran, ran, as
16 shots struck him on the back.
Wind across my window.

Wind across my window.
"I can't breathe", said Eric Garner
As the bow of the mountain

was wrestled to the ground
Wind across my window.

Wind across my window.
That motherfucking wind
Better start changing
Blues across my window.

Wind across my window
Two bullets to the heart Philando Castile;
Mistaken in Falcon Heights, MN.

RAKEYIA SCOTT: He better live.
        I swear, he better live.
Yep, he better live.
He better fucking live.
He better live.
Where is…
He better fucking live!

These motherfucking winds
better change!
Blues across my window.

Wind across my window.
Ex-Balch Springs police officer
Roy Oliver guilty of murdering
Teenager Jordan Edwards
There is a new wind
Across my window.

Let me hear you say it:
Michael Brown, Miriam Carey
Terence Crutcher, Yvette Smith
Philando Castile, Shelly Frey
Walter Scott, Damisha Harris
Eric Harris, Malissa Williams
Tony Robinson, Rekia Boyd
Tamir Rice, Shereese Francis
Laquan McDonald, Tarika Wilson
Eric Gardner, Kaythrin Johnston

GERARD ROBLEDO

A History of Violence

I

Yesterday, you shot a man in Ferguson.
His blood ran across the country.

Today, his people shot your people.
The heat from their mouths burnt a city to ash.

Tomorrow, someone else will shoot our children.
Covered in blood, you will wash, rise, & repeat.

Wind across my window.

II

Arrested, twenty-two-years-old, charged with public intoxication
& public endangerment. You keep asking why
they arrested you, while your last name echoes back
from others in lockup.

An officer tells you to *shut the fuck up,*
nobody gives a fuck about your rights.
Your rights fire back out of your mouth.
So, he & two other officers grab you,
they hammer across the back of your head,
& throw you into a 3x3 holding cell.

There you proceeded to urinate in your pants: handcuffed
behind your back, the metal scours your wrists
with every move. They refused to let you use a toilet
– they laughed.

III

Your wife gives you a book
which contains a history of political propaganda,

The Art of Persuasion.

Its text is black & white.
All you want is a cool tattoo.

On the cover: Hitler
holding a flag emblazoned
with a black Swastika,

encircled in white, and a sea of blood-
red cloth. Hitler bathed
in light falling from the heavens.

Inside: AMERICA FIRST!,
Churchill holding a Tommy Gun,
Yellow Japs; fists, cannons, & guns

pointing to the skies – facing East & West;
the Star of David, the KKK,

Native Americans painted red

with oversized noses & firewater;
Black men with swollen lips, hanging to the ground,

skin as black as the char on the crosses in their yards;
Finally, a section titled, "Propaganda for Peace."

IV

Eastern Promises: the film by David Cronenberg gives
an accurate depiction of life as a member of the Russian mob,

sex trafficking,
ultra-violence,
& the culture of tattoos
within the Russian mob.

Tattoos & criminal organizations are nothing new.

The tattoos that Hollywood actor,
Viggo Mortensen, wore
in the film were so realistic that

diners in a Russian restaurant in London fell
silent out of fear,

until he revealed his identity & admitted
they weren't real, the tattoos;
he was only acting in a film.

From that day on he washed the tattoos from his skin,
whenever he went off the set

the color from his skin poured
down the drain.

V

Your father isn't Russian,
he's just brown,

except for the majority
of his body,

      covered in fading grey-green placas.

You have teardrops on your face, & on your chest
a black hand holding the logo
E.M.E.
Too bad

when you go out into public & apply for jobs
you can't wash the color from your skin.

VI

When you asked the tattoo artist
if the bright colors will pop

against your skin,
she shuffled for a bit and replied,

*Well, it's harder to see details
& lighter colors when you have darker skin.*

So, for colors to really pop
& for the details to be seen

clearly, the lighter the skin the better.

GERARD ROBLEDO

To Brandish a Burning Head of Steel Wool

…charred body hangs from a chain in a chestnut tree in Waco, Texas, in 1916.
…a crowd of white men all dressed in suits and ties
and fashionable hats and stares
into the camera. One laughs.
— Steve Scafidi

807 people have been shot and killed by police in 2019

An unidentified person, a man armed with a knife, was shot dead
on Jan. 6, 2019, in Glen Valley, Calif.

California · Male · Unknown race · Unknown age · No/unknown mental illness · Knife

No body cam recording · Not fleeing
-Los Angeles Times

This involves flammable materials, it should be done outside / with a hood to envelop all the toxins. Tease the nappy wool apart / into delicate tendrils. Now simply set on fire. / You will get a nice red burning light show / – iron reacting with air to create iron oxide. / Steel wool burns vigorously when given enough oxygen, / and with enough heat it will become a self-sustaining reaction //

– a ceaseless flame. To make a blazing presentation / you will tie rope around the head of it / & give it a good swing / – make sure to give 'em enough rope / for their own safety. Divide the spectators: / keeping the children & parents apart; / distance them, they will each get their own ticket. / Pay no attention to the cameras, they will only distract you. //

Hold an acetylene torch to its end until it screams / a molten red drip, hot enough to ignite the worn ground / – leaving spindles of broken glass in your boot prints. / Crowds will gasp, a few may get burned, / so let them know you are in control. / They'll be safe if they follow the rules / & do whatever you say. / Make sure to stand behind this shield //

to protect your own flesh from any possible blow back / in the wind. Remember that you must first protect yourself / in the middle of this raging light show. This fettered head will swing / from your fists – a strange glowing red fruit. It will not cease / to perplex the foolish huddled mob that know the steel wool / will launch sparks that set nearby fires. Because this exhibition is too enticing, / their cameras will not cease to flutter, so let's go a step further //

for a larger flame. Distill bleach to potassium chlorate, it's pure white / powder form, and add it in masses to the steel wool. / It will burn hotter, brighter, and faster than ever. Just pass the torch / and keep it moving forward. Brandish the burning head / at your pleasure, its ashes will be washed away tomorrow and you can do it over again. //

CHUCK TAYLOR

Sandra Bland

I see my face in Sandra Bland -- let's pray that
Her's is not the only evil incident to shake me up,
But I see my lips, I see my cheeks, I see my smile,
I see my hope, I see my fears, my lack of faith,
my lack of surety -- something connects us
and that could be what it takes for care to
stick, that I see my face in Sandra Bland, or is
it that I am from Chicago too, that she's from
my home, that we did walk the same ground,
that we have breathed the same air, I could
watch the video, I could sit at home in my room
and watch it on the YouTube, Do I see my
face in the man who drags her from her car?
I have grabbed my own children who I love
that way, I have been filled like him with such
rage. Is this about being taught what's right
and what is not? Will we ever teach ourselves
what is right and what is not? I have driven
down that prosaic Texas road where she was
stopped. I was never stopped for changing
lanes without signaling, Many times I've been
to the school where she hoped to work. I know
what plantation used to own those lands where
the college sits I have walked La Liendo's
floors, that large and fancy house where some
see ghosts, I came not because it was once
a place of slavery toil but because famous

artists bought it after the civil war. It was hard
to find the plantation, many gave us wrong
directions. Sandra, you had such good hopes,
returning to your *alma mater* with the promise
of a job, I suspect they strung you up in your cell
but we may never know. Come back again
Sandra, come back to those who love, tell
us what you know. of what you loved and
what you dreamed, tell us what you hoped
to give, so to provide and make us happy.

CHUCK TAYLOR

The Grey Hole

I had a dream where a grey hole was swallowing everything.

    While in the dream I was fully convinced the grey hole was real and my heart was thumping as if the fists of the police were haranguing on
    my door.

My widescreen Technicolor dream of the world was far from perfect.

    The people I saw in crowds, some were smiling, but more were angry.
Many were fed but more were hungry. Some were calm but more were
    afraid, and many were desperately poor. The hole
approached like a giant mouth that was out to swallow everything.

    At times it ravaging the land like a capricious tornado, changing directions
as if blown by some force like a powerful wind.

People huddled together and held each other, people of every color.

    People sang together and prayed together and made music and recited
poems. People shot their futile guns into the grey hole but of course
    the hole kept to its capricious and ravenous behavior.

Then a voice started whispering like a bird singing in the distance.

    I struggled to move one toe, and then one foot, and then suddenly
my head shook and I sat up and was freed from my dream of the grey hole.

I searched around the room and I remembered where I was. It was the

Comfort Inn in Minneapolis! I had been marching the day before.
The sour aftertaste of the dream faded and I returned to living hope.

I ate what food remaining in the ice chest I'd brought with me from
our
    farm in South Dakota and headed out for more protesting. I knew
we had no use for ideology. I knew we didn't wish to overthrow
    the government. We sought by peaceful means to make lives better.
Some of us were idealistic. Many of us were desperate and idealistic.

MILTON JORDAN

Live P. D.

Martin L.K. Johnson, Booker Bonham,
Miguel Suarez and Pete Valenzuela
wearing baggy, drawstring denim trousers
over union suits fading to grey
and cheap plastic flip flops, standard issue
for a sheriff's department inmate,
stand three late afternoon hours along
the drive dropping to basement holding cells
beneath the county office building.
Three Saturday evening hours mark
the time their fifth crew member, Julio,
had before the hearse brought him up that drive.

MILTON JORDAN

Distanced Ritual

Burial bells at St. Theresa's sound
out now familiar tones as the Sexton
and a younger priest complete essential
services for the small family gathered
in masks before the pall placed early
by bearers in the newly opened section
of the graveyard still without monuments.

We join these near daily rituals
from our third floor apartment balcony
across Laurel Avenue, willing
our participation known to mourners
who seldom lift their gaze from the path toward
cars left idling at the gate beneath us.

-Michael Rothenberg, blood in the city at night

ERIKA E. GARZA

Cuando un policía muere

Cuando un policía muere
Se guarda un minuto de silencio
Se le hace justicia casi inmediatamente
Se le hacen honores
Se le llama héroe
Se le hace un mural

Cuando un policía muere
En el cumplimiento de su deber
Queda un vacío enorme
Queda una viuda
Quedan niños huérfanos
Queda una casa triste

Cuando un policía muere
Muere un esposo,
muere un padre,
Muere un hijo
Muere un hermano,
Muero un amigo.

Cuando un policía muere
El tiempo se detiene
Las fotos se mojan
De lágrimas tibias
Los uniformes se abrazan
Las insignias se atesoran

Cuando un policía muere
Muere un hombre valiente
Que dio su vida para protegerte
Muere alguien que se despide
Cada día de su familia
Porque sabe que está cerca la muerte.

ERIKA E. GARZA

When a Cop Dies

When a cop dies
A moment of silence is taken
He is granted justice almost immediately
He is given honors
He is called a hero
A mural is painted

When a cop dies
In the line of duty
An enormous emptiness remains
There is a widow left behind
There are orphans left behind
There is a sad home left behind

When a cop dies
A husband dies
A father dies
A son dies
A brother dies
A friend dies

When a cop dies
Time stays still
Pictures get wet
With warm tears
Uniforms are hugged
Badges are treasured

When a cop dies
A brave man dies
One who gave up his life to protect you
Dies somebody who says farewell
Every day to his family
Because he knows he is closer to death.

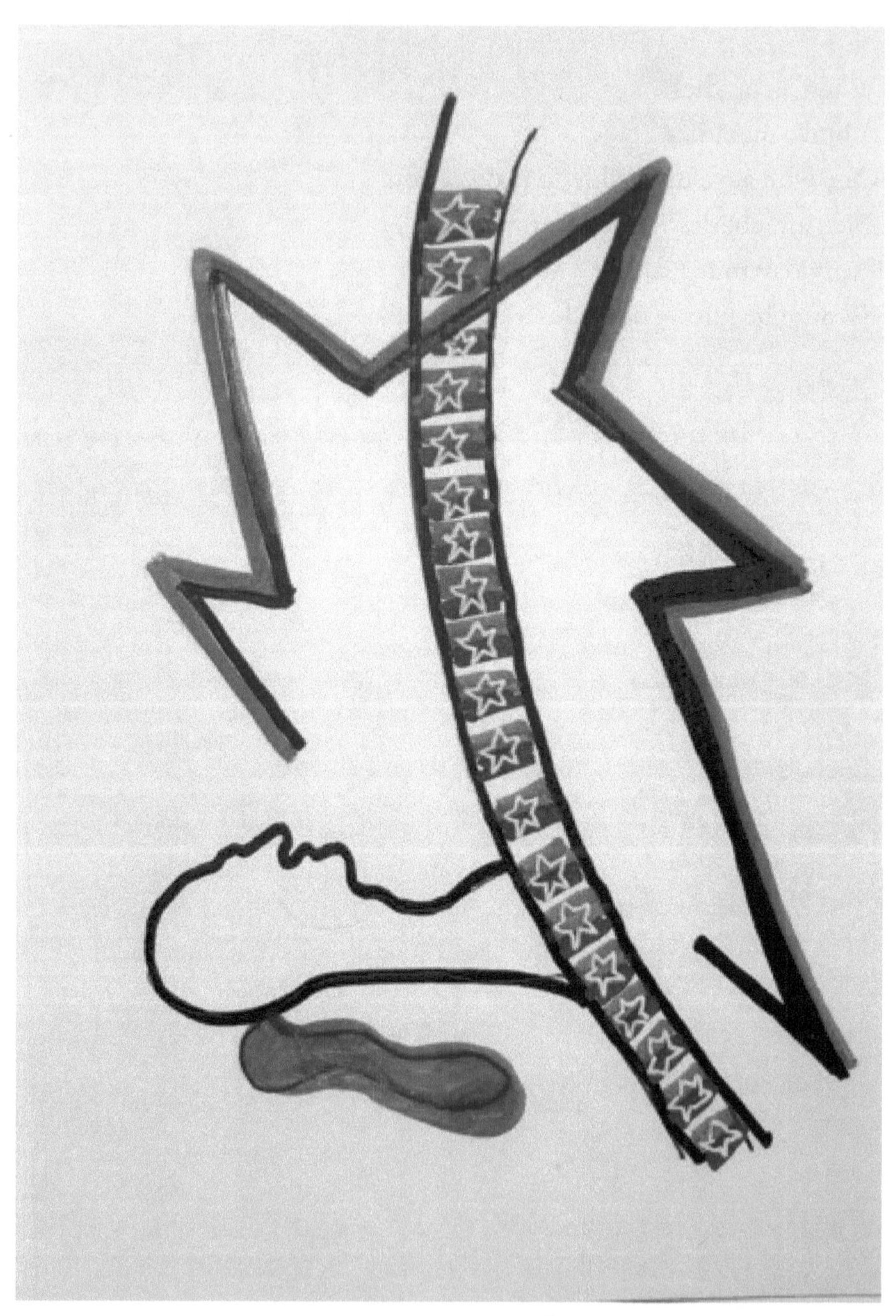

MICHAEL ROTHENBERG

MICHAEL ROTHENBERG

WELCOME TO SONOMA COUNTY

The monster beauty moon rises over vineyards
Apple orchards, and ancient redwood forests

*

It's simple. It was murder
Andy Lopez was assassinated by a cop
One bullet in the heart killed him
The boy fell to the ground
6 more bullets followed
Then the police handcuffed his corpse

Remember Oscar Grant, Trayvon Martin, Michael Nida, Yanira Serrano
Rigoberto Arceo, Kelly Thomas, Idriss Stelley, Ernesto Duenez, Freddie Gray,
Doug Zerby, Alan Blueford, Michael Brown, Eric Garner, Tamir Rice
all killed by police

5,000 people in the USA killed by police since 9/11
More than died in the Iraq war

Tranquil and retired valleys, prosperous retreat
There's no better place for good people to live
than Sonoma County

On Friday, the crowd chanted "Jail him now!" as they confronted riot
police outside the courthouse. An effigy of Sheriff Erick Gelhaus hung
from a nearby light pole. "You guys killed our friend, our cousin,
our brother," shouted Lisbet Mendoza, a Montgomery High student.
"He was just a little kid!"

Can poetry make death beautiful?

> *Just the few of us relax around the Russian River*
> *Mammoth rubbings on sea stacks older than Jesus*
> *Sea lions, vernal pools*

When they realized he was just a boy
Carrying a toy gun
They gave him CPR

A sheriff's deputy shot and killed a 13 year-old boy carrying a toy gun
A cop who fancied himself a gun expert, a war expert
A writer for S.W.A.T magazine
A skilled killer took only a few seconds to come to judgment
On the life of little Andy Lopez

Erick Gelhaus executed an innocent child
There's no poetry in that

> *Hot tubs and spas, vegan foodies and star magic*

When Gelhaus shouted out, Andy turned to his left and was shot through
the side, the bullet passed through his rib cage and severed his aorta.
According to police reports, it was eleven seconds between the time that
the sheriff called in to headquarters and the killing.

Arnoldo Casillas, the Lopez Family attorney said, "More crucial, in terms
of the incident was the amount of time that elapsed, between the time
the sheriff called out and proceeded to open fire. We do know that the
important sequence, the calling out a command to shooting, was just
2 to 3 seconds. The two women in another car behind the patrol car
said the cops were shooting as they were getting out of the patrol car.
Andy wasn't given a chance to respond or react."

We planted an oak tree in Andy's memory
A few feet from where he was murdered
All the kids pitched in and everyone, his mom and friends
Wrote notes to Andy and put them in the ground with the tree

One bullet to the heart
One bullet in the back
Another bullet in the arm
Two bullets in the buttocks
One bullet in each wrist
One bullet in the neighbor's fence

At 3:15 p.m. on a beautiful fall day in southwest Santa Rosa
Andy was going to visit a friend after school
He was carrying a toy gun

When he was shot dead by Erick Gelhaus

> *People here love their dogs, all kinds of poodles and doodles*
> *Lovely cats and agreeable parrots*
> *Occasionally, a boa constrictor*

If a civilian makes a mistake and breaks the law
They go to jail
If a cop breaks the law in the United States of America
These big strong men and women
These big strong cops cry and cry
How being a cop is a terrible job

A horribly dangerous job
They cry and cry and clutch
Their guns, their Tasers, gas masks
Bullet proof vests, armored vehicles, sniper rifles, bayonets
They cry, these big strong cops, they cry
Because they feel threatened by a little boy
Threatened by a little boy with a toy gun
They kill little kids because they feel justified
And they go free!

They cry
How they love their pretty families
Love their country, law and order!
It's a dirty job, they cry, but someone has to do it
They are our heroes, the brutes, storm troopers, corporate police
Claim they're making a sacrifice for the good of us all

Freedom, they tell us, has a price
Child murderers collect their paychecks
Go home to their pretty families

They cry
They don't have time to think about justice
Weak ideals like justice, no time for silly ideals like justice
These trained assassins want our sympathy
Want to keep us in line
Want to kill us

These tough cops
Cry for more money and compassion
They need more guns to be more effective
Need tougher laws to be more effective
Need protection from the people
We can't be trusted

The cops are the thugs
Gangsters and terrorists
They want more prisons, bigger prisons for us
To put us in our place, a place for us
Indefinite detention, solitary confinement
They want to control us
Because we don't respect them
We can't be trusted

We are ungrateful, out of control
They want a system with more bullets
More walls, more laws
They want to freely execute justice
Execute little boys with toy guns
On a sunny day in southwest Santa Rosa

Fall harvest time for the stinky buds
Compassionate use in peaceful towns

Murderers with badges in black and blue
Go home to make love to their wives and husbands
Blood on their hands
Caress each other in the bloody dark
Smear and smother each other in bloody love

With blood on their hands
The blood they want to call love
They play ball with their kids, cradle their babies
With blood on their hands
They walk their children to school

Bound by blood
Their bullets tear through
The hearts of innocent children
Just doing their job
They go home to their families
Kiss and grope each other

Hands stained with innocent blood
The blood they want to call love

The Sonoma Plein Air Art Festival
The Harmony Festival

Hearts rotten with angry justice
Tongues rotten with terroristic lies
Official murderers in black and blue
Who spend their working hours
Bullying the poor, black, latino kids
Anyone they want
Whenever they want
They are the law
Keep the law
Make the law

With a license to kill
They stop and frisk without probable cause
Strike fear in the hearts of us all
Just because they can
 "Keep the niggers down"

And we obey them
We are their niggers
Their field niggers
Their peasant jews
Still under the boots of robocops
They break down our doors

Beat us up in our homes
Answer our emergency calls for help
With a stick and gun and a fist
Rape us, kill us, break our bones
Murder our children
They are the law
These bullies with blood on their hands
Hate and fear in their hearts

"Kids will be kids," the cops say when their children get out of line
When our children get out of line they are assassinated

What a great morning for a hot air balloon classic!

Walking in our school clothes to play
Cowboys and Indians, cops and robbers
Just like on television
In our innocent daylight clothes
They shoot us dead

And when there's an outcry from the public
When a mother clutches the bullet-riddled corpse of her baby
When a father will never see his child again
When a family is destroyed
The police investigate the police
And the story ends there…

"I'm lonely living without my son," Sujey Lopez said.
"I need my son in my life."

The District Attorney, funded by cops, reviews
The investigation of cops done by cops
There is no poetry in that

Wild berry lanes, fresh crab at Bodega Bay
Where Hitchcock filmed the fantasy horror film "The Birds"

I believe there's a war against the people

Armed to the teeth
They tell us with stone eyes
The death of the child is "collateral damage"
The cops, the law and order folks
Cite extenuating circumstances
As they murder us in our homes
Bludgeon us on the streets
In our playgrounds and parks

This is how it really is
What will it take to get through to you?

The Luther Burbank Home & Garden
The Charles M. Schulz Museum

The police apologists say, "The cop felt threatened.
What would you do if you were a cop?"

The slavish apologists say,
"You would have killed that little boy too, right?"

Campaign fundraisers
Pasta feeds, crab feeds, pancake feeds
Calm and abundance, take a cooking class, play golf

"Jailhouse for Gelhaus!"
The murdering cop is on administrative leave
(Now he's back on the streets)
He will get his retirement bonus
Andy Lopez is dead forever

"No Justice, No Peace!"

Yes, you should have seen
The storm troopers at the Sonoma County Sheriff's Office
How they greeted our babies
Kids who came peacefully to demonstrate
Express their sadness and fear
About the killing of their little friend
They were greeted by snipers, behind barriers, tear gas
Brutality and force as an answer to grief
A lesson from bullies in the most teachable moment
This, their first lesson in democracy!

Blue jays, mystery-grilled mushrooms

California Sister butterflies in the morning
make you glad to be alive

*

We are purified by good actions, I say
I want my life back! I say
Will I ever find rest from this nightmare of police brutality?

One of Andy's friends screams, "Gelhaus, you will cry
like a Mexican baby when they lock your crying ass up in a
jail cell for 20 years"

What does President Obama think about the murder of a 13-year-old
boy?
He's too busy killing 13-year-old boys in Pakistan to think
about Andy Lopez

The apathy gene is missing in the sociopath

Gelhaus says, "turn on the mean gene"

While the wound is open we have to do surgery
The sickness is systemic, remove the rotten flesh
The shattered bone, punish the guilty
Cure the bully psychosis
Then we can focus on healing

*

Someone screams, "Fuck the police!"

And a child crosses the police line

Someone screams, "Fuck the police!"

Kids are getting beaten, harassed, shot by the police

Someone screams, "Fuck the police!"

A legitimate expression in the face of oppression

They are angry, yes, and have a right to be

Someone screams, "Fuck the police!"

Yes, a baby boy was shot in the heart
Two blocks from his home
On a sunny suburban day
Gelhaus was never at risk
He could have called in for backup
He was showing off

Andy Lopez was executed

In 11 seconds
Gelhaus got out of his car

Shot Andy Lopez 7 times
Handcuffed Andy's dead body
Gave the corpse (Andy) CPR
Then called in "shots fired"
In 11 seconds

Someone screams, "Fuck the police!"
Latinos and blacks and whites tell their true-life stories
Someone screams, "Fuck the police!"
No, I won't be winning any poetry contests with words like these
Someone screams, "Fuck the police!"
No lovely meditations on arrogant Renaissance constructions
Someone screams, "Fuck the police!"
No musings on gold tapestries and clever forms
Someone screams, "Fuck the police!"
No nice cupolas, no elegant verse and carefully placed metaphors
Someone screams, "Fuck the police!"

A father calls the police to report that his son stole his van
He wants to teach his son a lesson
But the boy would not heed the policeman's "lawful demands"
So the police shot him dead

Someone screams, "Fuck the police!"
Someone screams, "Fuck the system!"
Someone screams, "Fuck the president!"
Someone screams, "Fuck the corporations!"
Someone screams, "Fuck the military!"
Someone screams, "Fuck the politicians!"

And fuck the NSA who have joined us here for this intimate

moment of poetry. I know you are watching

No poetry with well-articulated parlor room niceness

Thanksgiving is coming soon
No, I won't be celebrating genocide

Someone screams, "Fuck the Mayflower"
Someone screams, "Fuck the Pilgrims"

It was murder. Andy Lopez was executed

Someone screams, "Fuck the police!"

Someone screams, "Fuck westward expansion"

And fuck what they did to the Plains Indians and the buffalo slaughterers
and the fucking Alamo

"Asesinos!"

Someone screams, "Fuck the Alamo!"
Someone screams, "Fuck Christopher Columbus!"
Someone screams, "Fuck the conquistadors for killing and raping
the Indians of Central America"
Someone screams, "Fuck the United States flag"
Someone screams, "Fuck all flags!"
And someone screams, "I don't support our troops"
Someone screams, "I don't support the *mean gene*"
Someone screams, "I don't support the 21st century Pinkertons!"

And fuck the police, fuck the president, fuck the prison industrial
complex, the military industrial complex, fuck the self-appointed
authorities of capital

Someone screams, "Fuck the slavemasters!"

We will not be painting the trees pretty colors
We will paint the air black with our voices

Under the redwoods and lush winter rain
After a Reiki massage and tabouli salad

Someone screams, "Fuck the police!"

There must be justice for Andy!
There must be justice now!

One freezing night in the Valley of the Moon
Candles and prayers, signs, more signs
We take to the street

I scream, "Fuck the police!"

*

The monster beauty moon rises over vineyards
Apple orchards, and the ancient redwood forest…

LINDA M. CRATE

so much work to be done

i see all these black and brown bodies
cut down by bad cops and bad calls,
and i worry about my Black aunt and my Black cousins;
will they be okay? will they be all right?
i don't know.
makes me sick that every time
i see a cop now
all i can think is: are you good or bad?
will you brutalize someone
or will you help
someone?
every time i see a cop,
i inwardly flinch;
cannot imagine how much more terrifying it must be
for my Black aunt and my Black cousins—
i want a better world for them,
for me, for us all;
it is exhausting holding your breath
waiting for the next bad thing that might happen—
how many people need to be tear gassed
at peaceful protests, how many people need to die
when they're doing nothing wrong?
how much is enough?
i am so tired, so tired, but there is so much more work
to be done.

LINDA M. CRATE

if you're going to be a brute

all these cop apologists
seem to have one thing in common
they're a part of the
all lives matter movement,
i've tried to dismantle that;
tried to educate my white friends
on how that is wrong and why it is
painful and unhelpful but some still
insist upon saying it—
why do all lives matter only when
someone says black lives matter?
i really need to know.
they say these good cops exist,
but they seem as mythical to me as
unicorns;
because i see the bad ones and no one
is keeping them in check—
police the police,
your badge gives you no right
to hurt or kill others;
it gives you no right to hurt anyone—
get over your obsession with power,
and the authority you want
over others;
i don't care how many years you spent in
the academy
if you're going to behave like a brute
that is what i'm going to call you.

EMILY SHEARER

The Silent World (This Poem Is Not About Jacques Cousteau)

Earth's cries echo underwater.
Everything we've done to deface her,
the sea's mirror. What happens down below, harbingers.

Dolphins, ancient oarfish, immortal medusas—
some say they can detect the fall of man
before man can show up for a stroll to the corner store.

The world erupts, silent no longer.
How can a flare burn so bright, so deep, so burdened
under all that weight?

Odysseus on the shore of Calypso's floating island,
Da Vinci of the deep,
reincarnates in a red toboggan.

By poring over a saucer, spilling tea,
 he flipped a system; he heard the drowning chanting
I can't breathe

and made a new lung, to ride or die on thirsty, salty backs.
Down in the trenches, life
eludes the aquanauts

who seek to unravel marvels:
what brine delights, how seamlessly sinuous skin kins
to oxygen and the element of Sol.

Meanwhile, barely keeping our heads above water,
we travel at speeds of haves and have-nots.
Can we narrow the wide gulf between two halves

and make one whole?
Where we bring to light the unfathomed,
shadows need not hide the truth.

Rumi says, You are not
a drop in the ocean.
You are the ocean in a single drop.

And everybody knows, the ocean,
the life force, the origin of blood and beauty,
isn't blue. It's black.

Notes

*1. Earth's Echo - the name of the youth environmental action group founded by
Cousteau's grandson, Philippe Pierre Jacques-Yves Arnault Cousteau, Jr.*
*2. Some jellyfish are called immortal because they can revert to their polyp stage in times of stress.
https://www.treehugger.com/natural-sciences/14-fascinating-facts-about-jellyfish.html*
*3. "The Silent World" - Jacques Cousteau's first book which was then turned into his first film, which
was the first documentary to ever win an Academy Award.*
*4. I was intrigued by the underwater flares the divers held during their early submarine explorations
and really did wonder how they worked. This, of course, is a reference to the incredible talents and
achievements of black people that have gone under-appreciated, neglected or abused under the cloak
of racism.*
*5. In The Odyssey, Odysseus washed up on the shores of an island where he met a beautiful en-
chantress named Calypso, who kept him imprisoned there for seven years. Calypso was the name of
Cousteau's research boat, purchased for him by a millionaire who rented it back to him for $1 a year.*
*6. Cousteau designed a vessel for deep sea exploration called the Diving Saucer. He got the inspira-
tion for the design from placing one inverted tea saucer on top of another.*
*7. He also designed the precursor to SCUBA equipment, an oxygen tank worn on the back, called
the aqualung.*
8. He referred to his scientific research divers as aquanauts.
*9. Sol - the Roman god of the sun; Sun; also Soul - soul food, soul music - traditional components
of African-American culture. Also the soul 10. A knot equals one nautical mile per hour; a unit of
measurement for speed traveled over water.*
11. Rumi - 13th century Sufi poet and sage
*12. This poem was originally written upon request for a collaborative art project between art teacher
Brock Gordon and student extraordinaire Connor Boone at fusion academy, The Woodlands, TX.
It was completed on June 8, 2020, which happened to be World Oceans' Day and the two-week
anniversary of the death of George Floyd.*

ERNIE BRILL

The Black Lives Matter Haikus

Trayvon Martin – Florida

I got my skittles.
Gonna see my girl.
Hey, man, don' point that at me.

A Note For Jordan Davis – Jacksonville, Florida

Watch your IPOD, son.
Wrong tune, dude shoots you.
You'll never listen again.

Michael Brown – Ferguson, Missouri

Hands high in the air
Police leave his corpse in the road
No one can touch it.

Freddie Gray – Baltimore, Maryland

Cops grab him for a long ride
He returns DOA.
What happened inside?

Walter Scott – Columbia, South Carolina

Scott shot four times in the back.

Cops deny the fact.
A bystander filmed the act.

LaQuan McDonald – Chicago's New Math

He's sixteen years old.
Cops shoot sixteen times.
Measure; solve for unequal.

Tamir Rice – Cleveland, Ohio

I like playing here.
BANG! GOTCHA! BANG! BANG!
Hi, officer. I was just

Sandra Bland – Hempstead, Texas

Stopped for a chipped light.
Insists on fairness hotly.
Found in cell hanging.

Lavish Diamond, Philando Castile's four year old step-daughter

Daddy point blank dying
Mother clenched crying
"It's o.k., Mama; I'm here."

Ballad For Eric Garner

Sells illegal cigs.

He's neighborhood known.
He's asthmatic. Cops attack.

He cries, "I can't breathe"
Struggles to be free.
Can't gasp past strangling chokeholds
NYPD bans.
Court rules against the murdered.
Blue perps go free.

Alton Sterling – Baton Rouge, Louisiana

He hawks used cds.
Cops arrive in parking lot.
No more sales. Ever.

Oscar Grant – Oakland, California

Can't make it tonight, baby.
At Fruitvale Station
This cop shot me dead.

Mother Emanuel Church – Charleston, South Carolina

No Amazing Grace tonight
For worshippers here;
Maniac slays nine.

Ahmaud Aubrey – Harwood, Georgia

Goes on daily jog.

Stalking vigilante guns
Ensure his last run.

Breonna Taylor – Louisville, Kentucky

Cops storm the wrong place
Friend defends; eight rounds
Pummel sleeping EMT.

George Floyd – Minneapolis, Minnesota

Clear murder all saw
Timid over-lying law
Into streets folks pour, roar, soar

MARK ANDREW HEATHCOTE

No matter a man or woman's colour

Televise the injustice of a man pleading for help,
and it's if we-too-have-also took a step back.
Eyes bat away like guilty culprits somehow impaired;
hand on heart-it's-eerie watching a man die point-blank.

Black lives matter, Lord, deliver justice-for-all
no matter a man or woman's colour, let no-man-fall
as did George, as did George Floyd this way again;
Lord, it's what we pray merciful Lord today.

Seconds tick—a lamb cries - I can't breathe, I can't breathe
officers "don't, don't kneel on any man's neck again."
Shouting, shouting, listen, "please, please, please", I cannot breathe
shouting "please" …while-onlookers plead, also shout in vain.

Seconds tick—and a voice dissipates like a-foghorn
time stands still as the world watches on with bated breath,
leaving an entire nation now to reflect and mourn
feelings of shared guilt, shock, a kind of mass, coalesce-

voice that—black lives matter, Lord, deliver justice-for-all
no matter a man or woman's colour, let no-man-fall
as did George, as did George Floyd this way again;
Lord, it's what we pray merciful Lord today.
Let every soul on earth corroborate-calibrate today,
so-this-awful kind of injustice never happens, again.

Lord, deliver justice for-all
no matter a man or woman's colour, let no- man-fall
this way again Lord, Lord, deliver justice-for-all
fair justice—as we're all sinners one and all after all.

GERARD SARNAT

1. HAIKU [5]

i. Just Ask Jalāl ad-Dīn Muhammad Rūmī (1207-1273) [3]

Curfew earlyed up,
jackboots on firebrands' necks,
what can word artists

do about menace
of unmarked police state thugs
pummeling citizens?

Here are our new rules:
break your wineglass. And fall toward
the glassblower's breath.

ii. i'm Down With This [3]

"In an effort to
promote Black voices, our press
is open for free

submissions for Black
writers in all genres for
the rest of the year.

We'll compensate for
loss of revenue, charging
you old white men more."

iii. Oy Risk-Takers Praise Be To George Floyd Memorial

Let's us have some church,
packed unmasked super-spreaders
break out in song, hug.

iv. Playing Ballsy [6]

Waiting on return
Major League Baseball's remnants
in long hot summer

are you depressed yet?
Pace yourself, this may be just
the very beginning

second-third inning
kvetch rather than celebrate
seventh inning stretch.

So lucky Prez self
proclaimed expertise ranges
from hotel buffets

to medicine to
Bible-thumping battlefield
commander -- to now

with unemployment
down not up, investment knack
tops Warren Buffett.

v. Mid-Septuagenarian Kemosabe's Last Round Up? [5]

Response to Sharpton's
profound George Floyd eulogy
-- untouched but unwound

casually racist,
Trump funeralizes Black
Lives Matter Plaza.

Watching same-aged white

protestor knocked to the ground
unconscious by cops

myself unmasked, I'm
moved to climb back in saddle
of social justice.

Message received: time
to deplatform Lone Ranger
poetry a bit.

2. TANKA* [2]

i. Worm Turns

Cop car runs into
non-violent protesters:
has The Big Apple,
once the world's greatest city,
become rotten to its core?

ii. Pandemic Hotspots

Seattle response
exemplary, WDC
LA, NYC
not to viral spread mayhem
after police slay George Floyd.

3. DELICIOUS NARCOCORRIDOS' LÍRICOS [3]

i. *Narcocorridos** Or Police State?

Hand in hand, toddler Liav
and I sang that song his eldest
of five first-cousin-brothers
made up with me when we
lived together in Redondo
Beach, "Walkin' in the alley
…talkin' walkin' in the alley
with Sally…"

Crossing Jefferson Blvd. in seedy
part of Redwood City -- few miles
from our family home of 36+
years -- where *Abba***/ Mommy
await our return for every-Friday
Shabbes dinner together, *boychick****
goes on and on about pre-school
friends 'n toys.

Post usual dose of Kitty Clinic petting
before feasting on one donut hole
(the Vietnamese owner/grandma
always wraps a free extra to "put
in your pocket then save for later"),
my senses are suddenly assaulted as
some nondescript van's siren goes off,
red-blue lights flash.

This culminates flagging over pickup
truck which initially does not seem
to understand what's going on until
an unmistakable bullhorn command,
STOP PULL TO CURB IMMEDIATELY
with black-uniformed apparent cops
jumping from their unmarked vehicle.
Oy oy oy oy oy oy oy.

 * Drug ballad in Spanish
** Father in Hebrew
*** Little boy in Yiddish

DAVID SALNER

A Short Poem on the Shooting by Police Of Charquisa Johnson, April 27, 2003, in Washington, DC

The police said she held a gun in the air
and refused to drop it. Her friend
said her hands were empty
except for the kiss she was blowing
her two children. They blew her lights out
but missed what was dangerous to them—
there it is, still blowing—
Charquisa's kiss.

DAVID SALNER

Three-Hour Reprieve
For Troy Davis (September 21, 2011)

A hard rain fell on the deck
and the recycle bin all night
as if the war far away had come
to our home, and bullets of rain
got sucked into the eaves
drowning us in the sound,
distracting us by the way
it slashed against our lives,
but by the time Barbara
and I went to sleep, they'd
already granted a reprieve,
a reprieve, which meant
they wouldn't do it to you
that night. The reprieve.
And it rained as we slept.
Downed limbs and puddles
and the muck of fall leaves
plastered to the sidewalk
greeted us by first light.
And the news—that guards
took you from your cell
to a room where you stared
at one-way glass then spoke
to no one you could see,
to us— "I am innocent...."
And it was your innocence

that the judges ignored
for three hours and more,
and it was your innocence
they tried to strap down
and shoot with a mix
of heart-stopping chemicals.

JACK E LORTS

Visiting Albany

Passing through Albany on the Coast Starlight heading for SLO, the young woman in front of us was getting a little mouthy, somewhat rowdy, flirting with the guy she was seated with. The conductor approached, tried to settle her down. She cussed him out, told him, "Go to hell." We saw him return, a little later, with an Albany policeman, ordered her off the train. She refused; the cop had to drag her off, not a pretty sight. Outside on the pavement, surrounded by Albany's finest, she was twitching from the Taser.
We think of this whenever we're in Albany.

(Reprinted from The Dribble Drabble Review #1)

STALINA EMMANUELLE VILLAREAL

Luto in Protest

"A policeman shot down a ten year old in Queens
stood over the boy with his cop shoes in childish blood
and a voice said "Die you little motherfucker" and
there are tapes to prove it. At his trial
this policeman said in his own defense
"I didn't notice the size nor nothing else
only the color". And
there are tapes to prove that, too."
—Audre Lorde

Spatial *WE ARE*
THEIR VOICES to show

a hatted hombre in uniform, murió
por ser él mismo. Say his name:

Joe Campos Torres. A veteran
imagen on a poster held

at the 3rd Annual Joe Campos Torres
Solidarity Walk for Past and Future

Generations. Racist police brutality
remembered. HPD beat and drowned

him. Remembered. ¡Joe Campos Torres
presente! He died on Cinco de Mayo,

cadaver found on Mother's Day.
Since 1977, la familia no puede festejar.

Now in solidarity with Black Lives Matter.
On poster, "WHAT

HAPPENS WHEN WE FEAR
FOR OUR LIVES?" Parent

and child abrazandose. Monica
Villarreal's printmaking captures

light, shadows, textures, gente
que sólo quiere ser gente.

BRANDON NISBET

No Knock

This is where we live,
where even the floorboards tremble with our history.
Where our shadows spread out like the roots
of a red pepper plant.

This is where we let sleep take us,
where we listen to the rain.
This is where we live,
And it will be destroyed.

No knock,
It will be destroyed.
Gun shots
It will be destroyed
A torrent of tiny trains.
I grab my gun—
trying to protect my loved one.
Screaming bullets split the air.
She screams
followed by
silence as thin as a strand of hair.

No body cams—
just a body.
No body cams—
just bullet holes.
No body cams just me

in the back of this pig's car
for trying to protect
my queen and castle.

After Stacey Waite (When the Dead Ask for Maps)
For Kenneth Walker and Breonna Taylor

JOHN C KRIEG

Eight Minutes

Say his name:
 George Floyd!

Monday May 25th, 2020
What happened?
They killed him
Who killed him?
Four police officers
One in particular
Who placed his knee on Floyd's throat
And brought his full body weight down
While the three others stood around
And watched it happen
For eight minutes
Overkill in the extreme
Because for the last
Two minutes 53 seconds
Floyd was already dead

Floyd died hard
Begging for his life
Saying for all to hear:
"I can't breathe!"
This proud black man
Who could have whipped any one
Of these tough guy cops
One on one in a fair fight

Called out for his mother, and
Finally made his final plea:
"P L E A S E ! ! !"
They didn't listen
They killed him, anyway

Wednesday night May 27th, 2020
Protestors burned a few buildings
And made it obvious that
They wouldn't let up
Until justice was served

Thursday afternoon May 28th, 2020
Justice was not served
As completely tone deaf
White mouthpieces held a news conference
And served up a word salad
The worst serving being when
The county attorney stated that the
Cop absolving evidence was not yet in
What the protestors heard was:
Bullshit! Bullshit!! Bullshit!!!
White mouthpieces spewing nonsense
Cowards one and all who thought
That they were in control
Of a seething rage about to explode
They thought that the protestors
Would heed their warnings
Because they said so
Because they held important positions
Because they were in charge

Because their white privilege was on high display
You will go along with *our* system
Because *we* said so
A prosecuting attorney only wants to bring charges
On cases that they are sure they will win
A human life was of secondary importance
To their conviction record
It's all about winning to them
Bullshit! Bullshit!! Bullshit!!!
Cowards one and all

Thursday night May 28th, 2020
This whole damn thing didn't have to happen
Although anyone with half a brain
Knew that it was going to
You could see it coming
Like a runaway freight train
Minneapolis is burning
I'm supposed to renounce violence of any sort
But it's hard to shed a tear for the demise
Of the cop's Third Precinct Police Station
Because like Pontius Pilate passing
Christ on to King Herod
They fired their own
But wouldn't arrest their own
Washing their hands they passed the buck
To cowards even more cowardly than them
Millions of dollars of damage
Done to innocent businesses
Apparently the white mouthpieces felt that it was
Better to let the town burn

Than to take on the cop's police union
America's President Donald J. Trump
Who we all know is lying
If his lips are moving
Threatened the protestors by Tweeting:
"When the looting starts. The shooting starts."
Gasoline thrown on the fire
By the racist leader of the free world

Friday mid-morning May 29th, 2020
The killer cop has been apprehended
While the three bystander cops
Are still at large
Too little too late
White privilege is now in flames
The raw nerves of Americans
Cooped up for three months
Because of the health pandemic
Are wildly throbbing across the nation
The country's eight minute snuff film
Is just too fresh in mind
The rage is just too intense
This outrage will have to burn itself out
In its own way, in its own time

A black man in handcuffs
With his face pushed into the asphalt
Begging for his life
Was killed in the streets
Of Minneapolis, Minnesota
In the span of eight minutes

By four renegade cops

Say his name:
George Floyd!

Cruel Cop, by Bob McNeil

BOB McNEIL

Text to Resurrect Revolution

Countee Cullen
And I are of this consensus:
Prejudice drafts psychopaths.
Their warpaths
Transfix our people to many a crucifix.
There resides the reason why
My protest must never relax
From typing its attacks.

Addressed to your psyche,
My compositions are microphones for
Emmett Till, Michael Griffith,
Yusef Hawkins, Amadou Diallo,
Sean Bell, Ramarley Graham,
Trayvon Martin, Darius Simmons,
Jordan Davis, Renisha McBride,
Eric Garner, et cetera,
Et cetera, et cetera.

Addressed to your psyche,
You can hear the murdered entreat:
"Don't allow another name to join
A homicide report sheet.
Don't allow another name to join
A homicide report sheet."

Addressed to your psyche,

The compositions
I've written are parts of a bulletin,
The passages transmit
To our terra firma's retina.

Addressed to your psyche,
My protest wants life
To evict the combustive
And discriminative.
If armed with you,
Lawfulness will live.

BOB McNEIL

The Blood on Blue

You have the right to remain silent
Until cruel cops harass you to speak.
You are warned that anything you say
Can and will be taken down and
Used as evidence against you, but
That excludes the Nazis in blue uniforms.

Some damn cops should be dropped.
Some damn cops should be dropped.

Nazis in blue hunt people of color.
Nazis in blue close doors to justice.
Nazis in blue say we resist arrest.
Nazis in blue think they're thick whips,
And we're naked backs waiting for pain.
Their badges are for spilling our blood.
Their uniforms are for filling our graves.
Some damn cops should be dropped.
Some damn cops should be dropped.

Nazis in blue, we won't disremember the names
Of those you wrongfully killed or maimed.
Nazis in blue, we won't disremember the names
Of those you wrongfully killed or maimed.
Nazis in blue, we won't disremember the names
Of those you wrongfully killed or maimed.

Some damn cops should be dropped.
Some damn cops should be dropped.

Look at the blood on blue,
Look at the blood on blue,
Look at the blood on blue.

JEFF CANNON

Yet we remain loving despite

night clouds attempt to cut the maiden moon from the sky, but
she returns to smile her gracious light, shower her night solace
over this troubled land, where sorrows grow a wild child homeless
terrified of itself in a world that no longer makes sense

yet we remain loving despite
the distance our lips must travel to deliver our heart gift to heal
what trembles within us, disturbs our sleep, further separates our
caring intentions from others for fear of getting murdered
knelt on while a blue being turned dark, prays a long prayer of angry
retribution for all those somethings that wander without names
only the growl of hatred

yet, we remain loving despite
sharp corners of hard winds, we caress, hold each other close despite
the electricity blasting all around us, hungry to kill us, since killing is
the answer to soothe madness, unleashed, by fools who believe they are
doing their god's good work

yet we remain loving despite
stand on the edge of life, bandage waterfall wounds, because it is the
only work our feeling bodies can do and we cannot make love
in a small room of our own seclusion while, such terrors masquerade
as goodness, reap harvests of vast profits, while the others of our bone
and flesh, blood, and life pulse, suffer needless death by being left
curbside to die in nameless gutter graves

yet we remain loving despite

we embrace each other, stand stronger together against the darkness
laughing while it burns everything of affection, human consolation of
recognition, give tears a chest to find a home for the lostness and fright
rumbling through that worn body about to take the top step of the edge
of despair, beneath them we stand together, break their fall into an
unnecessary oblivion, since we cannot save ourselves and lose existence

yet we remain loving despite

do not worry anguish, goodness is not dead, nearby small campfires of
its vitality glow to call you into those arms that have not lost belief in
care, we look into each other's eyes across the ocean, prepare to give the
all our bodily presence can give as the last offering, we cannot horde it
in our pockets, we were made to give, and so that will be our last
testimony if only the stars hear it and for the rest of their life bear
witness, we will not have lived in vain

RYAN HAVELY

For LC

Toss your flag on the top of the scrap heap
Don't get lost or cross the wrong back street
You might get tossed in the gulag or shot
By messiahs who mistreat you
Instead of washing your feet
There's a war in the streets and nobody's impervious
You have the nerve to ask me why I'm unhappy
While you're in tactical gear pointing your gatlings at me
Our fear is mostly practical
Our tears are flowing rapidly
You arrest us for our cheering
You arrest us for our chastity
You arrest us if we're curious
You murder us and hurry home
You've got dinner plans with your families

RYAN HAVELY

For BD

God's off tonight
As are most of his officers and prophets
Say your prayers to your lairs
Say em to your walls and your soffits
Claim to be righteous
Claim it right down to your pockets
Here our clocks feel pain
And our crops steal our rain
We're storing our insanity in boxes
Not a lobster from Maine
Or a mobster from the Bronx
Got a chance to repent; God's off the clock
Zip yourself in your tent; keep your soul tucked in a locket
Don't pay your rent. It's a pox on God's dementia

VANESSA CARAVEO

Weapon of Voice

I raise my voice
for the brown, the black,
the minorities,
the discriminated,
the outcasts of society
the voiceless.

Those who have been killed,
victimized, humiliated
for no other reason than for who they were born as
and what color of skin they possess.

No more!
Enough!

No more violence towards one another
rooted in hate and a false sense of superiority.
Guns are weapons that bring nothing but chaos and destruction.
Let us instead replace those arms of war by our voices
and let our voices be heard loud and clear,
near and far,

That we have had enough!
Not one more life lost because of hate and ignorance!

My voice will continue to echo throughout this world
and not for destruction,

but for *reconstruction*
of a better society for all
where one is not judged by the color of his skin
but by the substance of his heart and character.

Brothers and sisters,
we will not be silenced!
Raise your voices!

BRANDON JACKSON

Which Have Traveled Longer

Which have traveled longer?
Our feet or our tears?

Let us revisit the pain
Of a displaced people…
Walking through abuse for years
Took our African necklaces, and gave us noose
Ran for our freedom, from dogs cut loose
Took our royalty, and called us Nigger
On plantations paved, with cotton and blood
Raped our women but called it love
From gods to dirt
Enslaved to work the same Earth
We cultivated
Planted their babies, to our mothers' breast
Whipped God's portrait from her back
And beat the lions from his chest
Taught us self-hatred
Where black and brown is copied
but never celebrated

So which have traveled longer?
Our feet or our tears?

Let us revisit the rage
Of an erased people…
Marching through oppression for years

Took our insecurities, gave them lighter complexions
Ran for our freedom, from lawmen with guns
Filled our streets, with tape and blood
Killed our youth, called them thugs
But what's last, shall be first
And what's been silent shall be heard
Are you afraid
that we are angels reincarnated
To the same Earth we were slain
To make you face this light in us
That you try so hard to extinguish
By poisoning our water with lead
Or rejecting our stance to kneel
So you place knees on our necks instead

See my soul often wonders,
Which have traveled longer?
Our feet or our tears
Because my GOD, we have walked
And we have cried
We have wept for centuries in our stride
We stomp like giants in our belief
Shout loud in our praise
And moan through our grief
We stand tall
On ancestral shoulders
And wipe Nile rivers
From grandmother's cheek

Generations cry out
In times where cop shots

Are the modern day smallpox
We've had long walks on roads
With tears mapped out like an atlas of resilience
Cause I got Tubman in these steps
And Baldwin in my passion
I got King in my dreams
And Malcolm in my actions
Got Garvey in my movement
And Marley in my goals
Got a warrior in my heart and a peacemaker in my soul…
See, this truth and this love
Be too supernatural for human nature
cause Godly communication
comes from the roots,
from the hurt soles of mama's feet
to the shreds of daddy's work boots,
Because we must fight, rise and teach
We must run, jump, and reach
For everything Higher

Because we still been walking and crying
Still been marching and dying
And we
are TIRED

CHRISTIAN GARDUNO

8m 46s

The Scorching 20's have begun
One Law
Is it Washington, D.C.--
District of Columbia OR Department of Corrections?
Much too late for the Riot Act

1807 Insurrection Act
acting pious at Saint John's
Mobilizing U.S. Military Forces inside the U.S.
Dominate; beat the voters
Re-elect the looters
The CEO's in Patton Mode again
He loves tactical gear

Rally the base, blow up in your face
You can't control all the people all the time
Eyeball-to-eyeball with History
Is this all a show for the very few swing-states?

Flash bang tear gas
Night vision rubber bullets
The baton has been handed down
Every Generation must take its own beating
Archie Bunker wants to go nuclear
Demagogues within democracy
The money-changers have taken over the church
Insurrection indeed

Colonel Kurtz and the Attorney General
...on the Seventh Day, he crawled out of his Bunker
We are ending the riots and lawlessness
you can't have ANTIFA without FASCISTS

Remember when we demanded haircuts!
Social security medicare cuts!
Protect the Capitol and the Capital
What is to be done?

We must have contingencies
An ally of peaceful protests
& the 2A
This is what we're going through

Unite the People
Not just your own
Lip service rhetoric & tweets
A nation reacts out in the streets

CHRISTIAN GARDUNO

Sutures Breaking

Awaken the Pharaohs
this is happening, you know
when we all pitch in we share
King Tut's fixing to wake up

Yup yup woke
5,555 years since he last saw daylight
staying at the Luxor Hotel
awakened by the fall of the Liberty Bell

The end of us
is not the end of the universe
in the morning
the birds will sing for someone else

Phosphorescent white tungsten lights
yup yup don't let up
chasing leaves of light
learn to live another day

'92 with a Vengeance
(and the internet)
sometimes the system
needs its teeth re-arranged

No one ever told us we had it so good
Ah, let 'em riot

The City is shimmering
We're going into the woods

A claustrophobic catastrophe
no apologies or apostrophes
if you're lucky
an ampersand

Hey, let's never have a business-man as President ever again
that was miserable
you don't have to face the light
to feel its warmth

Very bizarre stars
sutures breaking tonight
your pain is the size of a pill
backwards up the hill

Locked in a moment of history
sealed in the amber archives
you can't just hope on hope
gotta go into the woods

History is such a buzzard
taking a knee won't do no more
100,000 Stores ain't even worth
one life

GABRIEL GONZÁLEZ NÚÑEZ

Manos de la protesta no. 13

*Poema ecfrástico a partir de
«Manos de la protesta no. 13»
del pintor Oswaldo Guayasamín

germinó
la ira
la ira que gira
la ira que todo lo mira
la ira que negra se estira

crece
la ira
la ira por los fanáticos
la ira por los políticos dogmáticos
la ira por todos los mentirosos automáticos

florece
la ira
la ira por los bribones
la ira por los malditos ladrones
la ira por los que acumulan a montones

estallará
la ira
en mil convulsiones
en un millón de explosiones
en el grito de mil millones de desesperaciones

ardará

la nueva Roma
de los comunistas y capitalistas
de los machistas y feministas
de los terroristas y pacifistas
de los laicistas y religionistas
la nueva Roma
de todos los istas

ardará

y desde las entrañas
de sus cadáveres hechos tierra
y desde entre los escombros
de sus murallas hechas ruina

germinará

tal vez

la esperanza

***

GABRIEL GONZÁLEZ NÚÑEZ

Hands of Protest No. 13

*Ekphrastic poem after
"Hands of Protest no. 13"
by painter Oswaldo Guayasamín

rage
has sprouted
a revolving rage
an all-seeing rage
a stretching rage

rage
grows
a rage against fanatics
a rage against ideologue politicians
a rage against compulsive liars

rage
blooms
a rage against the crooked
a rage against the damn thieves
a rage against the wealth hoarders

rage
will explode
in a thousand convulsions
in a million detonations
in the screaming of a billion desperations

it will burn

new Rome will burn
with its communists and capitalists
with its sexists and feminists
with its terrorists and pacifists
with its secularists and religionists
new Rome
with all her -ists

it will burn

and from the entrails
of her dead bodies turned into soil
and from the rubble
of her crumbled walls

what will bloom

will perhaps be

hope

DAVE RENDLE

No Justice, No Peace:
A Poem for Mark Duggan

I thought that all life was innocent,
but for some, this is not the case,
if you happen to be,
from the wrong part of town,
justice will be abandoned,
and deaths dominion,
will deliver to you,
a life sentence.

I can understand,
the undertows,
of rage and disbelief,
after bullets leave another,
young man dead,
and a mothers pain,
when her tears are washed away.

I perceive, recognise
the passion and intensity,
unleashed, after unwarranted,
bloodshed spills on our streets,
where certain hands that pull triggers,
are simply protected,
and that if you put your hands up,
authority might not want to see,
and why, when there is no justice,

there can be no peace.

*a poem written few years ago about a British Black victim of police injustice

CRYSTAL GARCIA

Daymare Destruction

My heart—
breaking over and over
and over again.

Simultaneously my heart remains enraged.
On fire along with the buildings all around—
maybe you feel it too or
maybe you're desensitized.
It could also be
you simply don't want
to feel the anxiety and
perpetual hurt this world
daily emanates.

Sometimes we prefer
the feeling of numb—
lately it feels like
gravity
is actually a downward spiral.
I understand that it can all
feel hopeless at times,
especially as I write this
during a pandemic.
All around the world
we are feeling sick;
either from a virus
or

sick of hate and senseless violence.

In the midst of the chaos,
the people must not turn a blind eye
to everything happening all around.
Protests turned to riots
yet who possessed weapons
and armor against the unarmed?
This feels like a civil war;
our streets becoming a battleground.
Not because the people do not want peace—
there is violence because power accompanied by
ego is corrupting.
We feel lost
losing each other
to the numbing pressure
of the heaviness of hate.

This weight we feel,
this weight that blocks
our airways—
we are feeling
this loss of consciousness
together.
We are feeling
the weight of humanity
literally bearing down
on our shoulders.
We belong to each other
so let's practice accountability.
We the People

must decide to rise up
or continue falling—
a divided nation
endlessly collapsing.

KAREN CLINE-TARDIFF

Still think this is the America we were promised???

Responses to George Floyd on my Facebook Feed

In 2010 police killed over a thousand people in the U.S.
WE NEED YOUR HELP TO STOP This!

I'm not saying that people haven't been killed by the cops wrongfully,
but this whole "white privilege" BS has got to be stopped.
Your responsibility to follow orders when a cop tells you what to do is
paramount.
Don't try to resist.

here's my white privilege:

The right wing is disgusted by this and we support justice for Floyd. We
do not support the looting or the burning but the right of the people to
assemble and demand redress and accountability of their government
is a shared cause.

you only care about the rights that apply to you.

Omg this is so cringe
Fucking pathetic!
you are disingenuous but you are in almost everything you post

It's from CNN Karen it's fabricated
race hustlers will be trying to drive a wedge into something that should
be the same cause

so being high AF is punishable by death?
These incidents are atrocities to the black race, they are atrocities to
mankind.

She went straight for the gun.
What's your point?
officers can murder people in broad daylight
They knew it then, and we know it now.

Thank you for not being afraid to post this

NDABA SIBANDA

Cut To Size

He---Mthethwa—would not leave a stone
of sham and shame sheltered by another.

He held a powerful pen that spat out
voguish reddish, scalding ink in the face of bias.
His words were saltier and sillier than satire,
more intense and poisonous than venom itself.
What they unleashed was a very volcanic thunder
bent on kicking their tomfooleries to hell.
His bravery tore apart the vile core of venality,
transmuted their blindness into alertness.
He galvanised their laziness into throughput
ripped apart their culture of prejudice.

Burnt to ashes were the bums of the felons,
cut short were the bristly tails of arrogance.

NDABA SIBANDA

Deadly Virus

This trigger-happiness
Is nothing but a tragedy
The wind blows against
A calmness in the face
Of deadly police brutality

NDABA SIBANDA

From Hogwash To Mouthwash

she was a lady who shared a great fellowship
that nurtured her as an activist and an educationist

at first, she embodied a spirit of softness and politeness
later her activism epitomized an ethos of civil disobedience

she delivered speeches that eulogized woman freedom stalwarts
like Queen Anna Nzinga of Ndongo, Winnie Mandela and Rosa Parks

is Rosa Parks not a heroine because she was tired of giving in?
she would ask rhetorically about the modern-day civil rightist

even days after the broadcast, she couldn't swallow it---
the bitterness of the verdicts, of the votes, of the statistics

the praise-singers and the public media fell over themselves
in a bid to sanitize and sugarcoat what was nasty and trashy

every day she yelled out names , words: boobs, badass, Bobs---
legacy, cancer, cholera, cruelty, crippling chaos, social chasm, curse!!

there was a huge group of citizens who dreamt and drowned in docility
they blamed everything on fate as they put up with the economic crap

I heard people plead with her, confessing they too were tired of the nonsense
she told them: shift from that kind of shit to grit, from hogwash to mouthwash

CONNOR ORRICO

Denying Defamation

Haiti pursues purpose while you perceive them worth less;
your perception is worthless till you see your blindness
to how they shine ultraviolent amidst ultimate violence
from ultimatums in private with U.S.-backed tyrants.

You is wack if silence to you
means nobody is crying.
Toujou somebody is dying,
ou fou si pa gade nou[2] trying.

Haiti is the world's winner, all black revolt from
slavery; the world is bitter, blackball insults
bravery, and world history books leave it out,
it aches me and the world you lie about so easily.

You just convene when justice is convenient,
justifying conflict with Justinian confidence,
judging communities not judiciously conversant:
that is less than juvenile competence.
It must go beyond conversation,
far beyond all your convolutions --
with 18th century conviction
they have engaged in revolution.

Haiti denies your defamation.

EL DAVID

THIS HUNTED LIFE

I am consumed
by this hunted life
I walk past troubled streets
torn, on edge
like rabid beasts
creeping through perilous land
on borrowed time /

The sight
of blood stained concrete
rattles me /
I now desire sanctuary
in dark shadows /
I want to shelter my pain
in chasms unknown
in tombs, ocean floors,
or padded rooms /
Away from constant threat/

I no longer wish
to drink from this cup /
Haunted by beasts
behind blood stained shields
Uniformed ghouls of prey
Tempt me to pass this torch
to drop this sword /

However,
I would rather not
be dried leaves
under deep bushes
trembling, fading
crumbling when touched
decomposing, rotting
into infested soil
doing nothing
to prevent ruin
becoming death /

These things
I do not desire /
I do not wish
to be passive and comatose,
one of the walking dead,
a face with no mouth,
living in chains,
embraced by agony /

But my skin peels
at the shrill of the demon's
banshee like sirens /
Red, and blue eyes
flash on dark faces
daring umber bodies
to test their eager fingers/

In solitude I fantasize
the nefarious scattering like mice

when my footsteps are heard /
chilling their bones
like the knock of the reaper
fearing the abduction
of their souls. /

I grapple with justice
with law and order
in places where cannons
watch through car windows
on blocks where overseers
silence hearts
where Goliath feet
stomp out David breaths /

Murals along my path
immortalize the victims
prematurely robbed
of their existence /

Hellish enforcers
Squeeze desperate souls
Into cramped corners
Unbalancing scales
Forcing fathers into reclusion
Color guards eat their own /
The children are left alone
finding fathers
in poisons and pistols /

I continue onward

two faced
loving and hating
right hand fist
left hand peace /

I encourage revolution
while advocating diplomacy /
white and black flags
fly above my head
and I hold hand
to heart for both
as I look out
to rubble and sufferings
These predators
open festering wounds
that never seem to heal /
I relate, unable to heal
consumed
by this hunted life

EL DAVID

ENDURE

These days
there is something remarkable
about a Black or Brown man
that dies in his home at peace /

There is something amazing
about justice served
when the abuse of power
robs guiltless men
of their heartbeats /

These days
there is something exceptional
about a Black or Brown mother
that sheds tears of satisfaction
to the sound of a gavel
crashing down
marked by the word
GUILTY! /

It is spectacular
when the Sunday suits
of Black and Brown men
are last worn standing
instead of lying down
cold
in afforded caskets /

These days
It is amazing
that we still have composure
That we have not
lit this world on fire /

That the angry
have not exacted
violent upheaval
and retaliation /
Blood for blood
son for son
heartbeat for heartbeat
breath for breath /

It is remarkable
amazing, and spectacular
that we continue
to march forward /
that we continue
to hope and dream
still believing
in a better tomorrow /

That we
through bullets
and glass ceilings
through blind juries
closed borders and slaughters
remain strong

remain intact /

It is amazing,
but true
that we…
endure

DANIEL GARCÍA ORDAZ

I'm Gonna Need You To Calm Down!
(Ensure Domestic Tranquility)

Be still and know
that I am GAWed.
Guaranteed an annual living wage under the law?
Oh, hell naw!

No law is the exception:
Laws passed by the rich come with great expectations—
under-the-table motivations,
back-room deals, sleight-of-hand interpretations
purposefully-passed with built-in imperfections.
Please excuse all the exceptions made just after the election.
(Not available in all states—for your protection.)

People in the line of duty aren't often held
responsible for their lack of civility.
Yet people in the sights of a gun are required tranquility?
In the face of hostility?
Calmness amid calamity?
Deference in the face of indifference?
Cool charisma in the midst of chaos?
Rational thought in the throes of rioting—
while the self-righteous mock lootin'
in a highfalutin voice?

Do we even have a choice?

If you don't want to face a jury
(not of your peers,)
embrace not the fury,
or you'll be serving years.

Lead lessened lives of quiet desperation.
Bury the hatchet of frustration,
Do as you're told by manifest destination.

It's up to you to ease the tension.
Settle down or never make it to a pension.
Retire in the penitentiary for crimes of habitation
in our nation, crimes based on the color of one's skin—
remnants of slavery, segregation: prejudice, discrimination.

Revolving prison doors don't reflect evolving mores.
Scores and scores of men deemed rotten,
left to mold as misshapen forms, begotten
directly from a sinful seed—so evil,
they're reared to explode generations of upheaval.

NANCY SHIFFRIN

Space Flight 2020

Black Man Murdered by police in Minneapolis
peaceful protest devolves to riots
Gucci Beverly Hills looted
my favorite bakery reopens
I once again buy lavosh
where a homeless encampment inhabits
the sidewalk adjoining the parking lot

Synagogue Vandalized
President calls out National Guard
we observe curfew
our friends zoom and facebook and youtube
what does the omniscient omnipotent benevolent
Deity want from us
is the Holy Spirit no longer our Friend

Astronauts reach the Space Station
first privately funded launch
will there be martial law
will there be an election
whom shall we follow
has the world gone crazy with cabin fever

Douglas Park
rangers remove some of the ducks
try to educate the children
I am afraid the ducks will choose

another place to breed
can we properly mourn George Floyd
can we be grateful to everyone
holding up a sign to ensure his memory

will we move beyond the abyss

MARK ESPERANZA

Could it be true?

It is said God's children man-up!
– and so we do.
We praise balance as all and
do as we did when we
stood full face before the judge

– that day

at the courthouse

when we dropped our countenance
on cue
as per script
and tapered the specter testament
one lone true-self –
not the deviant-soul they themselves fathomed out of device
but this –
what is left of us.
This you see before you now.

Could it be?

– they say it is what it is.
How they crept after us
through our infancy
sentenced to life-forfeiture beyond the veil.

Could it be true?

Some say it is true
the fated rubric of collateral weight cannot lie
they say
and so we turn to memories divided
of crowded days in drastic solitude
and the orange cloth
how they all agreed
then
that day
when they
turned red-ignorance to wine
and said,
It's your own doing, and
Serves you right!

And with days upon days
piled on feathered days
atop severed days
with ma' at a close distance
watching
our chained days under the gaveled veil –
– was it true – as they say?

Could it be as true – as they say –
– as on the day of the crucifixion?

– that day

beyond the stone they chose

to rectify their own salvaged death with —
— beyond the stone they chose
to pass over and fortify themselves against.

Could it be
as they say
it was those committed to the murder He was really after?

Such is the truth of the stone rejected
we know
now.

Yes.

Days upon
days of death and ascension,
we all know now who played what part
in the Great Passion Play of our times.

O, day of days,
this our near savage birth

— listen closely

for the truest verdict of our time
lurks
just beyond the shadow-depths of this stone veil.

Oh, yes.

God is near.

M. GERLEMAN

My Voice

A distinctive foghorn, cutting
through background noise,
my own private public address
system, a sonic blast produced
by an oversized head, a megaphone
made of flesh, bone, and cartilage,
my voice has served me well.

And I have put it to use! My opinion
is never kept to myself. I know a
lot and am not afraid to show it.
My voice alone wins arguments
and conquers foes with its
wisdom and judicious reasoning
(or at least its volume).

But now, it is time for me
to be silent. I must silence my
own voice to hear the cries
from the streets, from the parks,
from the young who rise up,
from the old who say "not again"
from the people whose own
voices have been dampered,
voices that have been misunderstood,
voices that have been ignored,
voices that have died out,

because society has placed its
knee on the neck of those
who only want us to hear them
say, "I can't breath".

I am listening. I am waiting.
Please tell me what to do.

MEGHA SOOD

An Act of Self Defense
After Ahmaud Arbery

The exact moment when the grief takes
shelter in your heart and leaves you undone
when the emptiness sits in the gaping hole
an abyss of loneliness:

the deafening lull in your mind stops making sense
the only loss which makes sense
are the lonely wails of the widow
on the apartment above you

Sorrow takes a different shape
when your tear starting pouring
for the senseless acts of violence and cowardice
carried by the very educated hands of this land
where life, liberty, and pursuit of happiness are
foundations of society, the sidewalks of those
are now pitted with the black bones of their own

You are not carrying your freedom in your arms
/your right to bear arms/
when the only right you have given to a mother
is to stick a cross in the middle of an unknown street
giving a piece of land for her dead son
there is nothing but death at the end of a gun

When the names keep adding to the unnamed list

Treyvon, Michael, Eric....and so on
an ever-growing list of the dead and forgotten
where names have to scream out loud to
make their lives matter or else hell will break loose

To hell with your right to the Second Amendment
when it's laced with the blood
of a black brother whose murder
you are incessantly
trying to justify as self-defense

MEGHA SOOD

A Nation in a Chokehold

Yes, the streets are overcrowded
Yes, the lanes are bustling with protest
Yes, there are streets thrumming with anger
overcrowded bus stops, sidewalks, bike lanes, parks
brimming and spilling with pain
Unfettered;
Uncontrolled

Everywhere now should be quarantine
where the lanes should be deserted
where everyone should be *six feet apart*
masks covered mouths but still breathing
with breaths laced with privilege

Here the nation recalls the pain
the unanswered angst of those calling from the grave
for those grieving souls who are yet to put at rest
those headstones, now a place maker for a black mother
to sit and cry alone in the deep folds of the night

Here the nation mirrors the screams
of the black blood lacing the sidewalks
mouth gaping at the nakedness of the whole nation
staring back at the end of a gun a *police gun*

Here the nation acknowledges the police shooting went awry
here the nation recalls how the protectors devour

here the nation recalls how easy it's for you to forget
a loss of life and wait for the next news cycle to begin

Here the nation recalls how eyes pop out
losing life in an instant---
when your brain misses the next wave
of life-giving air coursing through your veins

Here the nation recalls how the brutal hands
loaded with power thick as greed,
dripping with incessant hunger
took lives boisterously

Here the nation recalls how life was ignored
leaving the warm and supple body
on the sidewalks pitted with fear and blood

Here the nation recalls how to survive
by sucking in, gulping air
taking deep long breaths feverishly
trying to survive after being
in a chokehold for 8.5 minutes

Here the nation remembers Eric Garner
Here the nation learns again how to *breathe*
Freely!!!

MEGHA SOOD

Peace - a metaphor for denial
Winner of the Spring Robinson/Mahogany Red Lit Prize

Peace, an act of ignorance
an act of denial is not a bliss   *no more*
when the silence is gutted like a fish
and the blood of your own fills the street.

How long can you be the puppet
in your own peaceful country?
the act of abandonment speaks a muted language
for all the hearts trapped like sparrows
on the other side of the town.

The wall creates a boundary between me and humanity
they are still considered illegal with one foot in my land
another bloodied and stuck in the barbwire
that I put around God's own country.

I was born with a privilege
to call the piece of earth I was born, as my own
No matter it is laced and seeped
with someone's else blood
it belongs to *me* now

The young boy is shot
the pavement is colored by the color of his blood
dark and useless;
to the people of this peaceful country

those who pull out the armrest and the beach chairs
to see the stars lit up the sky
and the deafening noise
muting the wails of a widowed mother.

They sip the beer as cold as their souls,
leaving the scene with a shrug and a short sigh.
Ignorance is bliss. Peace is a *metaphor* for *denial*
In this country, I call mine.

MEGHA SOOD

Bless Us Lord for the
Sin-Free Life We Are Living
First Published in the "Lift Every Voice" by Kissing Dynamite

I stare with my gaping mouth
mock and revere
at this whimsical reality
eyes rolling in disbelief
head bowed in silence
knees scraping at the pew
to absolve my sins

We only bow down to the fear of the unknown
the fear of being punished
by an exalted god in heaven
carved in our faith
surviving generation
through reams of yellow-tinged holy scriptures

Surrounded by a million slithering tongues and roving eyes
flooded by the shining spotlight
waiting for it to become a trend
to become a sensation,
for the ignorant minds to be aware
of the writhing pain
it has to catch fire and burn.

Leaving marks on our suppurating skin
seething with blisters in pain of losing

a loved one,
a life,
a country,
an identity.

It takes a million to march and protest on the roads
the sun scratching their faces
burnt and scathed by the injustice
screaming in silence
gutted like a fish in the open streets
thick blood staining the curbside
Of the lands we boisterously own

The nakedness of humanity
staring in the gaping hole in his chest
shot in the broad daylight
in the middle of the goddamn market

We turn our eyes in shame
moves our heads in disbelief
and thank our gods in heaven
to spare our loved ones
the ones we love--
the ones we really care

We move with our twisted spine
towards the house of gods
to worship the one sitting in heaven
to suck away all our pain
and bless us with the sin-free life
we desire---a life in vain.

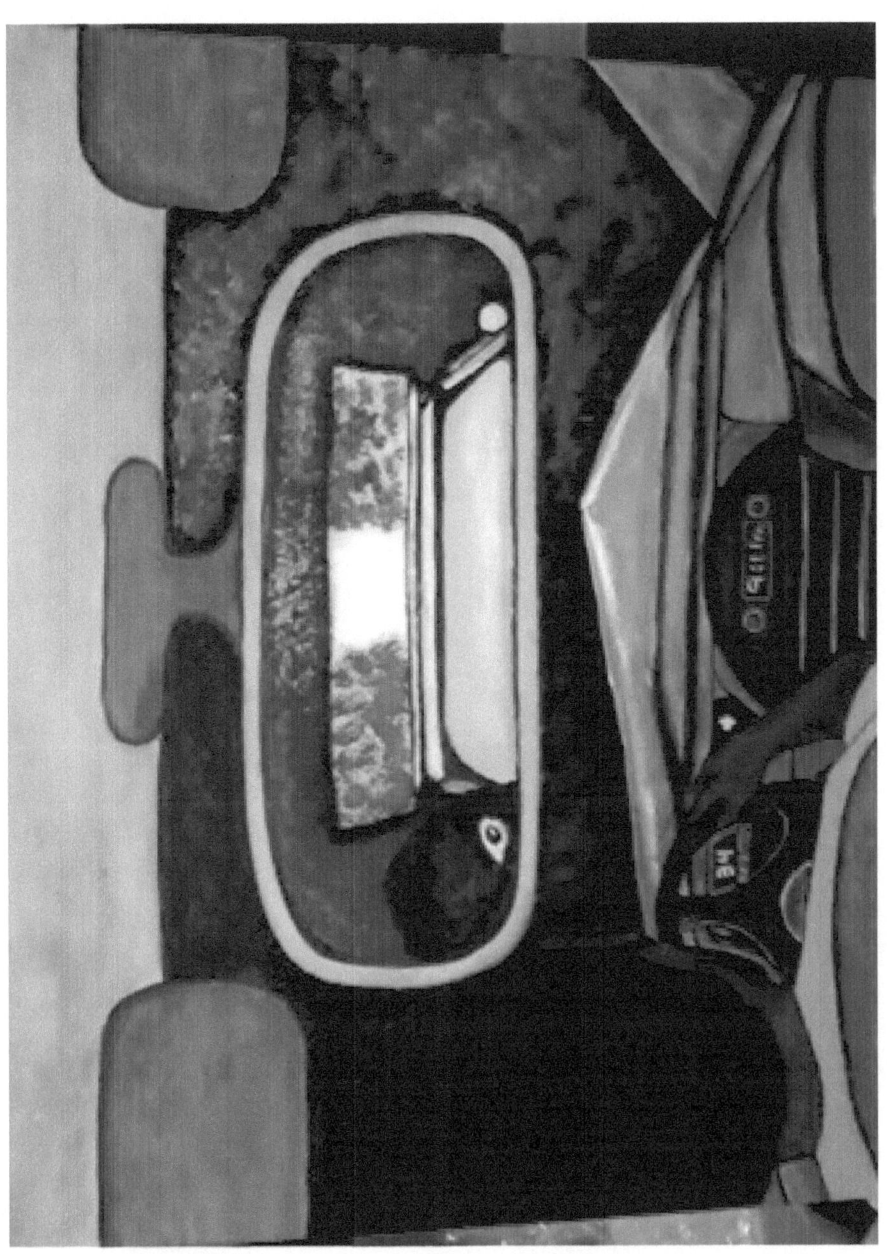

MARK LIPMAN

Sticks and Stones
for Brendon Glenn (Dizzle), killed by LAPD, 05 May 2015

(whisper): Sticks and stones
may break my bones
but the police
are out to kill me. (x3)

Sitting alone
in a cold, damp alley
nothing but stars
above me.

Here come the lights
all shiny and bright
sirens and badges
they haunt me.

Hands in the air
and down on the ground
they're pulling their guns
and though I'm unarmed
and pose a threat
to nobody,

they come to shoot me down
just because of my poverty.

(whisper): Sticks and stones

may break my bones
but the police
are out to kill me. (x3)

If you're black or brown
or homeless in this town
they throw you to the ground
the verdict is already guilty.

If you're a suit and tie
you turn your back and lie
making money while we die
shutting your ears to our story.

(whisper): *Sticks and stones*
may break my bones
but the police
are out to kill me. (x3)

We throw our hands in the air
saying "Don't Shoot," don't you dare.
but the politicians just don't care
they only serve and protect the money.

So don't act all surprised
when the people begin to rise
and call out all your lies
this is the voice of the many.

(whisper): *Sticks and stones*
may break my bones

but the police
are out to kill me. (x4)

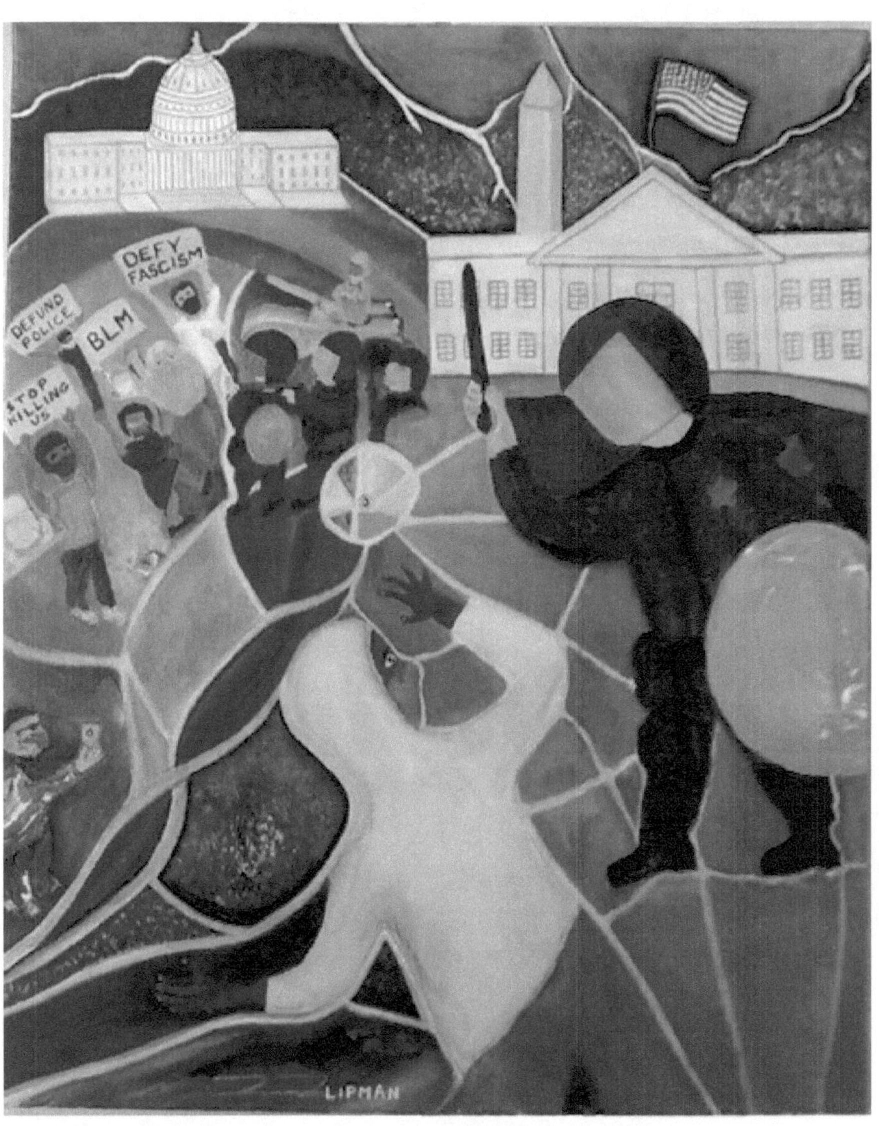

DEFUND POLICE
DEFY FASCISM
BLM
STOP KILLING US
LIPMAN

JONATHAN FLETCHER

No Room for Human Error

A white spacecraft is launched.
A black man is pinned to the ground.
This mission is a test.
This is not a test.
Observers record the launch.
A bystander records the arrest.
The spacecraft leaves the atmosphere.
The man cannot breathe.
The spacecraft loses gravity.
The man loses consciousness.
The astronauts arrive at the station.
Paramedics arrive at the scene.
The astronauts remain with the crew.
The man remains motionless.
The spacecraft is shuttled back to Earth.
The man is shuttled to the hospital.
The mission is pronounced a success.
The man is pronounced dead.

MARTINA GALLEGOS

I Ain't Met a Good Cop Yet

My sister who suffered from mental health issues
became disoriented in the middle of the night
and walked aimlessly in hopes of finding help.
Minutes later, a police car approached her
and asked if she needed help. She said yes.
Once in the back of the car with one of the pigs,
started making fun of my scared sister,
and the other pig joined in the miserable fun.
The pig next to my sister started fondling her,
and the other animal laughed his ass off.
My sister regretted having accepted such 'help.'
She was too scared and traumatized to even report the incident.
Never trusted damn cops again.
Thanks a lot, Oxnard PD!

I was a university student having my day off from work
in my apartment and was all alone, too.
Suddenly, I hear loud banging on the door, and I hurried
to see who it was but didn't have much time for that.
Before I knew it, a bunch of cops had busted the door open.
They wanted to know who else was home
and didn't believe I was alone,
so the pigs proceeded to turn the entire apartment
upside down, tables, sofas, beds, and busted into
every room without even blinking.
Needless to say, they never showed a search warrant,
but after they'd turned the apartment inside out,

they got a call that whoever they were looking for,
lived on a different street altogether.
All pigs busted out the same way they busted in.
The entire apartment complex was surrounded by pigs.
No apology necessary, thank you!
This is how Northridge cops roll.

One of my brothers was walking home from work
on Halloween night, and he saw a bunch of thugs
mess up somebody's Halloween decorations.
Some Seabees were in the area and must've called the cops
because they showed up very quickly and stopped
my brother and started questioning and harassing him
about the damn spooky decorations.
He insisted he hadn't done anything and pointed
to the direction where the hoodlums had fled.
Cops called my brother a liar and started beating him up,
and before they were finished, they'd busted his back,
and now he can't hold a job because of his back pain
thanks to the Hueneme cops.

My older brother was driving home after his job
when he got to a light that was green for him to go,
but a lady on a bicycle ran a red light, causing my brother
to abruptly apply the brakes of his produce van.
Unfortunately, he couldn't stop on time and struck the lady.
He called 911 and waited with the lady till help arrived.
He drove behind the ambulance to the hospital
where cops were quickly interrogating the critically
injured bicyclist in the surgery room and my brother
in the waiting room, but my brother was able to speak to the

nurse who was present during the questioning of the lady,
so my brother went home in peace.
Two years later, two detectives show up at my brother's
house, with a warrant for his arrest for murder.
The unexpected news couldn't have devastated my brother more,
and he remembered what the nurse had told him,
that she had run a red light, and he had actually tried to avoid
hitting her, and that the accident was not his fault.
It was obvious the pigs left that crucial information out.
My brother insisted on getting in touch with the nurse who'd
witnessed when the cops questioned the lady,
and he kept going back to the hospital and talking
with anyone who'd listen.
Eventually, and miraculously, he found the nurse who testified
before a judge and told him what the lady had told the cops:
It was my fault. I ran a red light and he did try to stop.
Crooked Pasadena cops lied and almost sent an innocent
person to rot in prison, but this incident still destroyed his life for good.

My abusive neighbors kept damaging my property, stealing water
and electricity to grow pot when it wasn't legal, breaking my sprinkler system,
and parking a huge truck in my damn driveway just because they could.
One day I heard a loud noise and ran out to check and saw that a young
driver had wrecked my mailbox then drove away.
When he walked back I told him what he'd done, in case he
didn't know, and I told him he'd run away. He said he'd only
parked across the street, a few blocks away.
He quickly went in the house, so I went to speak with, my bad,
maybe I shouldn't have because a raging cow opened the door
and told me I couldn't talk to the driver because he was a minor,
and that was child abuse, interesting...

I told her what the child had done, but she quickly told me to
report it to my homeowner's insurance, ok, lady, who wasn't
even the owner of the house.
I called the cops and waited by my doorsteps while the mail came, too.
When the pigs arrived, they quickly brushed me off and headed next door.
Should I close my mouth now or wait?
When the cow came out, the cops greeted her respectfully and inquired
about her well-being. I'm fine, thank you, oink!
The mail carrier arrived, and I was walking to the mailbox,
but a sow quickly squealed and yelled at me to stay back!
And his freaking gun was out of his holster and in his hand.
Cliché, cliche, but I saw my life pass right in front of me,
and this wouldn't be the first damn encounter I had
with creepy Oxnard cops…

Photograph by Edward Vidaurre

EDWARD VIDAURRE

reason I don't own a gun

I don't want to go out the Hemingway,

you see?

Who will tell of the stories, the bloody ones?

Blood trails, inside
the stomach of the hanging tree
hold voices
of strange fruit

innocent prisoners
tell a truth that leave an iron taste on lying tongues

But let's talk about the moon

Moonlight, liar in solstice, who will uncover her true light
if i go out the Hemingway?

A

Witness to dream-crossers
Poets with riverbacks, never wetbacks, only setbacks,
always wading in slow running water,
waiting in compact spaces
for the trigger happy boys to drive away,
away,

Away, far away,

go
away!
   ¡Ay Güey!
But not the Hemingway

I need to stay,

to tell on the oligarchy? to bleed on paper?

I don't own a gun!
I don't want to be blamed!
I don't want to be your terrorist!
I don't want to be your brown man killer poster child!
I don't want you to break down the door to my sacred space!
I don't want to be on a documentary on the anniversary of my death
and your death and their deaths.

I will keep knocking with my voice, sometimes I'll get loud, sometimes
it'll sound like thunder, but it won't be a gun!

For my *dead cold hands* will be clean of blood. It's my words that will
pierce through.

HABIB ABODUNRIN ZAKARI

SHALL THE LAW SPEAK OF THE BLIGHTS

For souls taken by police brutality

Shall the law speak of the blights
The abusers who hack at sanity
Wrenching souls with the long arm of unreason

shall the future turn a blind eye
as innocence get pummelled
how much kicks can truth take
how much life shall strangulations yield

shall weakness be way-laid,
at the lone boulevard of callousness
Is sunset meant for falling at dawn

shall the land trudge on
on dirge of threnodies
would tomorrow find hope
in skewered justice

MICHAEL BRAUTIGAN

Undisclosed

I remember the chalk outlines
that looked just like us

the city rolled me, rolled me one
and I smoked it

and when the girl I was waiting for
saw me
her face lit up like a jack-o-lantern

I remember some people lived in
apartments
but we lived in houses

they lived where kids got run over
by freight trains
and got on the news

then our next door neighbor
got shot and killed by someone when
he answered the door
there was a police ribbon across
our driveway

soon after my parents sold the house

MICHAEL BRAUTIGAN

Holes Everywhere

poverty holes
despair holes
misery holes
dishonesty holes
hatred holes
ignorance holes
denial holes
complacency holes
crippled holes
unloved holes
violated holes
hidden holes
forgotten holes

THOMAS FUCALORO

The Four Boroughs

Before the quarantine, no one wanted to come here

Then they built an outlet mall and an invisible Ferris Wheel

And then people came to the tip

On the NYC subway map, we look quarantined and boxed in

What keeps people away

Is it the distance

In our ideologies

That shrugs us off

Or is it we

In the Urban Dictionary

Staten is defined as

An adjective used to describe something guido

Or overly trendy in the image of the Staten Island style-

The borough that wishes it was part of NYC but just isn't

And then separation anxiety travels by ferry

And I am not sure where I live

I pay New York City taxes

And care about New York City

While being *just isn't*

But the real problem is

That *I am*

And what others get to do

Is shit on an island

Trying to not understand the through-

Way

Expected to travel

To get to me

Is filtered by you

And I hate Staten Island

And I love Staten Island

And some of us are racist, misogynistic, homophobic, and transphobic

But so are some in the other four boroughs

And like New York City

We try to engage the racist, misogynistic, homophobic, and transphobic

Staten Islanders

And help them understand that though

I am a Staten Islander and I am proud

I am a Staten Islander and I am angry

But no one is looking to hurt you

Be a part of the movement

North Shore vs. South Shore

Is all bullshit

Staten Island is in a fight for its soul

And that soul, today, is focused

On the lives of black Staten Islanders

Who we know are

Staten Island

And the fact that you won't

Fight for Staten Island

Has put us in a sort of quarantine

From Staten Island

I'm not a New Yorker

I am a Staten Islander

And only a true New Yorker

Understands what that means.

NDABA SIBANDA

Denouncing, Dismantling And Discarding The Chains

What people experience becomes their story and history--
Including persecutions and prosecutions and other perpetrations
No prescriptions from any power can erase such experiences
By virtue of the fact that people are products of their environs
By the same token people are at liberty to write about what they
Feel closely connected to, or concerned about, or outraged about
They should not be shackled, but should tackle what has to be done!

NDABA SIBANDA

Shocking Complicity

it is good to be write or hype hoarse
about an optimistic future and course,

it is commendable and fathomable,
ignoring an injustice is unconceivable;

to encourage the pen to overlook
it is to exhibit a deplorable look,

 a feel-good song that sanitizes bias
is hollow, hurtful, suspicious and impious

BONNIE PRICE

I.C.E. (In Case of Emergency)

I read some shit the other day that made me trip
The article read, in case of a nuclear fallout I should have a survival kit,
For 3 days, I should have enough water, foods, and meds
Prepare to take a dump in a plastic bag,
Secure my freedom papers in an airtight container
You know for just in case,

I laughed.

If the Notorious KIM decides to flip the switch and make America its bitch
There won't be enough water to baptize the remaining survivors
Because they'll all be Handmaid Tales

They say in an emergency dial 9-1-1
In case of fire you may bust the glass, grab the axe to survive by any means necessary,
Yet how do we survive being black?

Where's our kit?
More importantly, what's inside?
If such an anomaly exists, I'd say it looks a little something like this

Determination and strength to endure scrutiny and prejudice
Repellant to stave off incoming racists
A mask to disguise the anger with a smile
While Officer Friendly and Make America Great haters continues to profile

Three days of fasting and prayer to overcome unwarranted stares
A pin to prick my blood to prove
I'm human just like you
Sealed with an embrace from our ancestors
The original investors in our future
And a map created with scriptures
When you don't feel safe
To lead you to a sacred space

Brothers and sisters, keep these things with you
Guard them with your life
When the emergency comes, I need you to survive

EMENIKE CHRISTIAN CHIJIOKE

I CAN'T BREATHE....(a light fades)

"Please I can't breathe.
My stomach hurts.
My neck hurts.
Everything hurts.
They're going to kill me."
This was Floyd's outcry.
Eric Garner cried alike
Before they choked life out of him.

I can't breathe....
When you sit on my rights
And ignore my screams
Simply because I'm black.

I can't breathe....
Because the stench of your hatred
And the coldness of your heart
Are threatening and murderous.

I want to live.
Is that too much to ask?
As air has no color,
So does life.

Let's come to light
And bridge this racial divide.
Allow blacks to breathe;
For our lives matter, too.

JON C. MANNONE

Five Vignettes on Racial Hatred

1. Montgomery, Alabama
The National City Lines, Bus No. 2857
Thursday, December 1, 1955

Rosa Parks steps onto the yellow
& green-rimmed bus, stops to make
sure it's the Cleveland Avenue one,
drops the coins into the collector,
and sits down. The driver notices
through the rearview mirror, glass
stained with spit of epithets, tells her
to get up for the white person.
But she stays determined in her seat
looking straight up to the white
ceiling for some solace, some answer
to prayer, but only the flies buzz
under a canopy of hate-filled breaths.

2. Birmingham, Alabama
Trailways Bus Station
Sunday, May 14, 1961

The stopped bus at Anniston was allowed to limp away
on slashed tires; peaceful protestors said prayers. But
in Birmingham, the bus was battered even more with clubs,
bats & pipes. Policemen conspicuously absent. The mob

smashed windows, blocked doors, threw fiery slurs
infused with a gasoline bomb. Trapped human beings gasped
on the floor, black-smoke-stained glass left as shards
of violence. The innocent crawled under the canopy
of choking chemicals only to be kicked and punched
in the heart as much as to their heads and torsos.

3. Birmingham, Alabama
16th Street Baptist Church
Sunday, September 15, 1963

The bus stopped to let
the reporter man off to see
the stained-glass glass stained
with children's blood, a dark
cloud canopy of hopelessness.

4. Charleston, South Carolina
Emanuel African Methodist Episcopal Church
Wednesday, June 17, 2015

Some waited at the bus stop,
rushed to a prayer service
in a Charleston church to find colorful
stained glass fractured with lead
bullets from a Glock semi automatic.
And they themselves, too.

A canopy of angels cried when they

couldn't guard against the inhumanity
when the roof came down on their prayers.
Dylann Roof, a white supremacist,
mass murdered nine African Americans
in hopes of starting a race war.

5. Minneapolis, Minnesota
Just outside Cup Foods Grocery Store
Sunday, May 31, 2020

The 17-year old clerk looked at George
with jaundice-stained glassy eyes, suspected
a counterfeit-twenty for a pack of cigarettes,
called the cops to Chicago and East 38th.
Outside the red canopy of the store, police
knelt on George Floyd's neck, it was Sunday.
The crowd prayed out loud, yet the spirit
of the man rushed out of his body in less than
eight minutes and forty-six seconds, whisked
away with bus exhaust from a passing metro.
It wouldn't stop.

~ ~ ~

When will hatred stop burning?
When will the burning hatred stop?
When will it stop—the burning, the hatred?
Will the hatred ever stop? This burning
Hell, is it destined to continue?

JON C. MANNONE

Long Walk to Freedom

> *[A]ll persons [should] live together in*
> *harmony and with equal opportunities.*
> *It is an ideal which I hope to live for ...*
> *But if needs be, it is an ideal for which*
> *I am prepared to die.*
> — Nelson Mandela, 1964

The faces of freedom come in every shade:
Moses, Miguel Hidalgo, Abraham Lincoln,
Geronimo, Martin Luther King, Mandela—
Fighters of bigotry

Evil has no boundaries, but *can* be confined
with kindness,
confiscated to a point of nonexistence,
replaced with love,
for we do not fight against flesh and blood
but against the rulers of darkness

Rifles can kill the body, riddle it with bullets
leaving a wake
of fire, smoke, tears,
but the mouth, loaded with guile,
can kill the spirit
Foul words leave a trail of devastation
with a fire of hatred, smoke
of deceit

We must forget the guns, but shoot down
the politicians
with the honest words from sacred texts;
let them bleed out their anger
And we will bleed with them
—we are all connected. There is no true myth
so powerful that it blurs the realities

One might say Mandela is a *secular saint*
Let us all distribute
the wealth,
not that of diamonds,
but of something more brilliant:
Forgiveness

Now we can *move past the past.*

---

*Italicized text in the second verse is cited from Ephesians 6:12; all others
are quotations from Nelson Mandela, his close friends or commentators.*

JASON D. SÖDERBLOM
AMERICA'S REFLECTION

When brutality and death are whatnots. Collateral to a rancid plan.

To humiliate the victims. The police state reigns again.

When pleas for breath are laughed at. When rule of law has faltered.

Do you look at South Africa's apartheid years?

And can you see the reflection in the window

AMERICA GARCIA

A Movement, Not A Moment

A reminder that we need to be in a collective effort on what we're fighting about and on what we're experiencing.
We need to know your history on anti-blackness, systemic oppression, privilege, and the role you and your community in upholding systems of white supremacy.
We need to educate family members about African roots in Latin America.
We need to bring visibility to black folks.
We need to support organizations and activists that are fighting for this movement.
We need to support policy changes that could help combat structural racism in politics.
We need to read up about anti-blackness in communities.
We need to take action to step back and ask questions with all these resources being shared all through social media.
We need to defund police to invest in healthcare, mental health, trauma services, housing, childcare, education, and employment opportunities.
We need to stop being afraid of being wrong.
We need to stop asking black people to educate you because they're not required to.
We need to get uncomfortable.
We need to use our privilege.
We need to acknowledge how we spend out money to support this movement.
We need to destroy myths.
We need to amplify by sharing black stories, black art, and black voices.

We need to stop cultural appropriation.
We need to stay updated on continuing action.

DAVID ROMERO

A Pig at the Door – For Yvette Smith

There is a pig at the door
Threatening to blow our house down
Huff-puff
Someone called 911
Claiming my son had a gun
Deputy Willis didn't question it
A Black household
We used what we had to build these bricks
But they thought our family was made of straw
They say the law is the law
But it sees what it wants
And justice is blind inasmuch
As it can close its eyes
My son and I used to play hide and go seek
1…
2…
3…
Ring around the Rosie
Cops and robbers
I didn't bother to tell him
Because, to him, it was obvious
How many see us as prey
Cornered targets
A 911 call
The opening of a door
Can quickly become an emergency
A pig arrives at our threshold

He should go away
Know that an argument in this house
Can blow over
With a gust of wind
Huff-puff
He comes to knock our house down
Huff-puff
Huff-puff
Bastrop County, Texas
My name is Yvette Smith
I am survived by a boyfriend
A son
Huff-puff
How many more homes will they blow over
Huff-puff
With their lies?
With their guns?

DAVID ROMERO

Hands Up, Don't Shoot – For Mike Brown

Darren Wilson
You'll tell reporters
Tell the world
When they question
Why you did it
Why you killed me
You'll say,
"It
Looked
Like
A Demon"
You will take my life
Then deny me my humanity
Post-mortem
Make me something monstrous
A justifiable homicide
Murder by cop
You will make me something monstrous
A statistic
Another one
Criminal
Thug
Gangster
"Did he have weed in his system?"
"Any known gang affiliations?"
You will make me something monstrous
Black buck

Mindless beast
Rampaging monster
Demon
You will tell them
About the brimstone emitting from my nostrils
You will them
About the flames dancing in my eyes
You will describe
The horns on my head
Pointing at your chest
You will appoint yourself
Judge
Jury
And executioner
All because
"It
Looked
Like
A Demon"
Officer Wilson
I am not an "it"
I am a young man
I am not your demon
I am a human being
When the bullets fly and I fall
It will be human blood
They will find
On this street
My neighbors will bring candles
Keep vigils
My family

Will weep
Let's go back to when
My hands went up
Like a white flag waving
"Don't shoot"
"Don't shoot"
Let's go back to when
My hands went up
Please holster your gun
Take out your handcuffs
Or wait
You called for backup
They're coming
They're coming
Don't shoot
Don't kill me
Officer Wilson
My name is Mike Brown
Don't make me into another one
A martyr
To a cause I never volunteered for
You'll say,
"I know you robbed that liquor store
I know you have those cigarillos in your pocket
You're no angel"
No
I'm not
But both sinners and saints alike
Have been granted miracles
And remember
Jesus hung with two criminals

He promised them the kingdom of heaven
No, I'm no angel
But a choir of them
Somewhere
Right now
Are kneeling
They're praying
They're saying
"Hands up
Don't shoot."

Photo by James Schwartz

JAMES SCHWARTZ

"Old Order Supremacy"

How will I use my white privilege & body during this time? Racism in the Old Order — let's destroy it the way Jesus drove thieves from the temple, flipped over tables & brought big dick hardcore revolutionary energy to his Divine Work.

Topple systems of oppression that will usher in a new heaven & new world. No justice, no peace, defund the police. The kingdom of heaven is within our autonomous zone.

Anabaptist ancestors, hear our cry: Black Lives Matter. Amish bishops: "Birds of a feather flock together" is a racist as fuck response.

Ecclesiasticus 27:9 is just the tip of the spear. White AmeriKKKa cherry-picked the Bible to justify slavery. True story bro. Try Jeremiah 22:3.

 "I don't want black men in my house" an Amish man once hissed at me: my father, after I brought home a trick from the club one Saturday night. I laughed at dad as we left & went to his apartment in Kalamazoo for sex & shots. House music night & I am the only white body on the packed dance floor. Frankie Knuckles mixing with sweat & gin & northern heritage. He holds me close, our kiss defiant.

Amish can go their whole lives without seeing a person of color…

CATHARINE BATSIOS

We are Running Out of Options

I.

Or, We Should All Be Horrified
because "anonymously-state agents"
who black-bag people into delivery vans
is utterly—to the point of nonsensically—
immoral. Sludge. It's an extreme escalation;
to strive to invoke fear in a population
that wakes up dead
is ripping off our costumes strip by strip
until *we see* that *you know*
we have nothing left to lose. We are
running out of options, hold tightly
to your hearts & your friends.

II.

People to call if I disappear:
Someone to speak of my present heart,
one to notify the network of my blood,
another to bring in the family.
I missed most of my teens & 20s
trying to get through my teens &20s,
call someone who can say *mission accomplished*
& smile for me.

Reasons I might disappear:
I spoke
I saw

I threw in my body to save one
Reasons I won't disappear:
I will hold on for reasons other than me
I am waiting
I am hungry for/starved of a sense of self
Reasons I want to disappear:
I both do & do not exist

III.
This may not work for you
if you've never stayed in bed
from the first 'til just before the last alarm
to *convince yourself*
that you're still alive &
the only affirmation is,
don't want to be late for work,
but we are running out of options.

LAURIE KUNTZ

Darnella's Duty

Darnella Frazier is the brave young woman who filmed the murder of
George Floyd on May 25, 2020

How does it feel to be 17,
and just want to hold your life in your
glistening palm, go to the corner
and buy a sparkling water to quench
a parched mouth that longs to sing?

How does it feel to witness
a purpose too cruel
for all your 17 rotations
around a sun you only want to bask in?

How does it feel to beg a name,
witness a life breaking,
while your opened ebony eyes,
see loss and corruption corralled
to the borderless sky?

And, how does the humid wind feel
as you watch it carry one man's life
to a crevice where only the wind can go?

JAMES CROAL JACKSON

My Privilege

I'm privileged to sit in my home on a sunny day
with just a headache
in late May two thousand twenty. God I feel
plenty guilty. My friends
are linking hands in the street and I am scared
of all that's viral. Oh what has lingered
in the air since, yes, America.
I have wept with internet videos
in my shadowed home,
never gassed
standing up for what is right.
You say *protests are only one part of the revolution. We can't*
just go out there and put ourselves and others in danger.
How does that help the cause?
I am donating fucking money
waiting
for unemployment to salvage
fruit. I can't say no
to a food bank donation. To
the Freedom Fund. Reclaim the Block.
Justice for Ahmaud, Breonna… If I am not
downtown with my people
burning businesses of bigots
take all my worthless fucking money
and light the biggest fire
possible

JAMES CROAL JACKSON

I have been having nightmares of a police state,

of walking down the street at night, red
and blue sirens wailing past, and people
being shot in front of me, their bodies
dragged across the sidewalk
out of view.

Maybe because I've binged
The Handmaid's Tale
or worked too much (stress
the swan song we stay singing).

Whatever the cause,
I live
in America, America,
America.

PEGGY LANDSMAN

THE READINESS IS ALL or THE FATAL SHOOTING OF EULA LOVE BY TWO LAPD OFFICERS ON JANUARY 3, 1979 IS STILL UNAVAILABLE ON VIDEOTAPE

-published in *Calyx* in 1995

Eula Love, Hands cuffed behind your back as you lay in your blood, Shot
eight times—waiting two-and-a-half hours for the ambulance To arrive.

Why didn't you pay your gas bill on time?

The collector came, said they'd have to turn off your gas. You flew off
the handle, hit him with a shovel. Not hard enough to hurt him, But
enough to make him run....

Meanwhile, you ran— To the corner store. Bought a money order to pay the
damn bill. You had babies you couldn't ignore, didn't want them to suffer.

The cops came—their guns out, their guns aimed— Enough to
make you run, screaming, into your kitchen Scared out of your wits.
You must have been their worst nightmare—some bitch screaming,
Threatening to turn armed men to jelly.

You grabbed a butcher knife, wielded it wildly, But finally threw
it down After they refused to stop pointing their guns, After they
refused to start listening to you.

You just wanted to tell your story: You lost your temper, you were sorry;
You should have paid on time, but you only just got That $22.50 together.

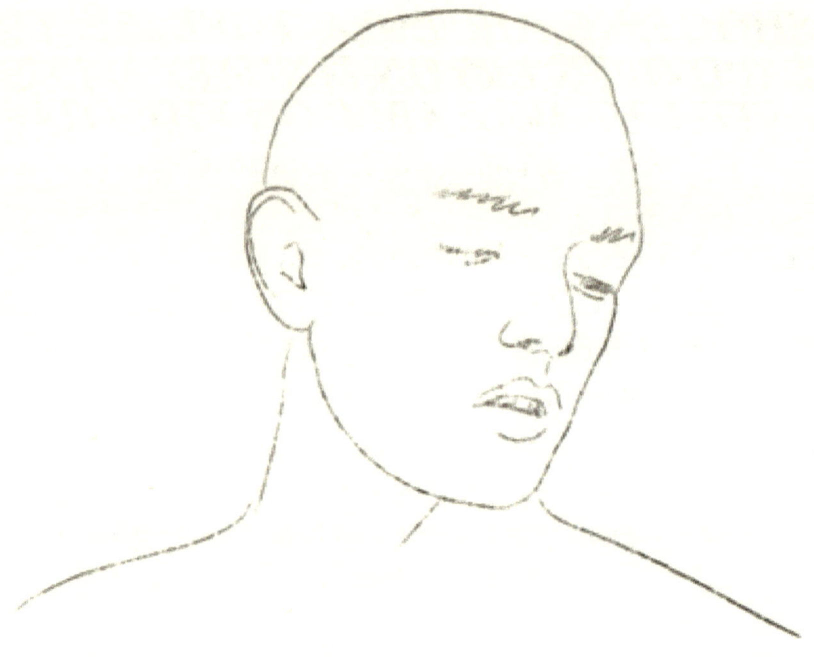

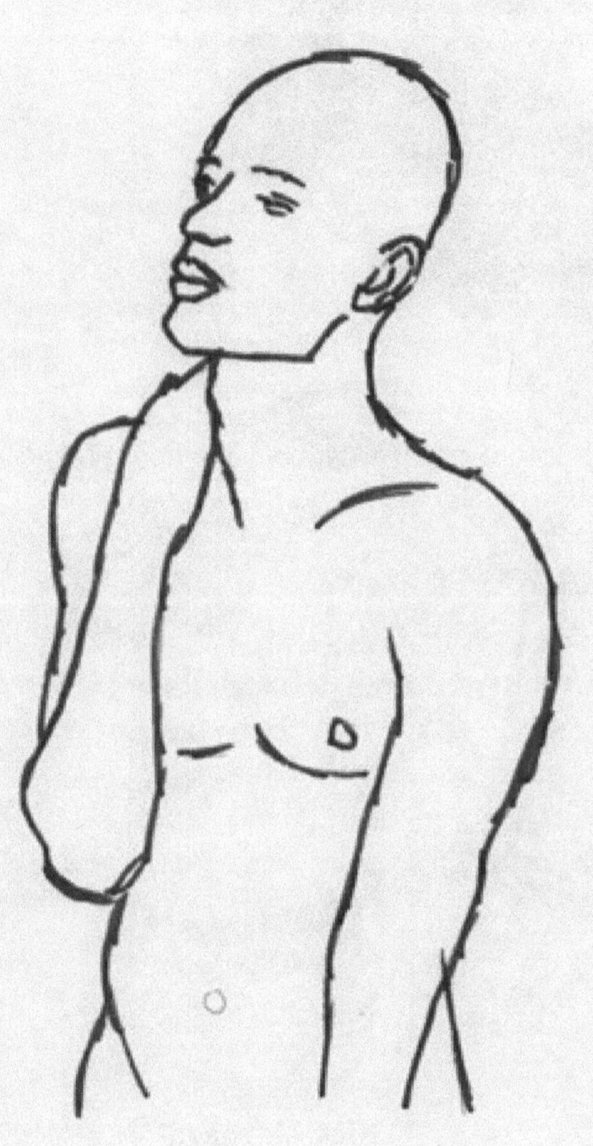

Nick Maynard

RONALD K. CRAIG

A Long Journey

burning desire to vote
the piddling fire hoses of
Birmingham

a phalanx of troopers
daring to move
at the foot of the bridge

Black Lives Matter
peaceful protesters cross the bridge
every day

long journey
from "whites only"
to the end of the rainbow

police officer
skill set . . .
free kick in soccer

the gulf
between protesters and police
riot gear

skulls cracked
in Selma and Portland
history repeats itself

taking a knee
not giving one . . .
good cops

John Lewis
crossing that bridge one last time
bright sunny day

June 4th in China . . .
still asleep
in America

JEFF KNORR

One Night

But not just any night,
on the 26th floor of the New Otani Hotel
the night of your aunt's wedding
your new uncle and I threw centerpieces,
beautiful flowers in glass volleyball-sized
vases out of the window of their hotel room
in downtown L.A. We dropped them, in
amazement, the air flattening petals of roses,
the baby's breath. They blew out
like cannon balls on the sidewalk—
flowers, soil, Styrofoam, glass. Ten times
we could have killed someone with one of those
centerpieces, our drunkenness—
it could have been over as soon as it started.
Your aunt's anger flared hot as a brand.
We could be wearing the same prison orange.
I escaped some wild death, manslaughter
by wind, by stupid luck, but you on the other hand
drive the car through our neighborhood,
stop for a cigarette with friends, have brown skin--
you ride, get pulled over, the cops
looking for you and your brothers.

JEFF KNORR

Father Fire Blackbirds Wind Son

If I could clean your heart, release you
like a wing-shot pheasant catches wind.

Catching the roar of fire and wind,
I closed my eyes, looked toward the sun.

Looking toward the sun the confused father
is trapped in the heat you know as your own fire.

Trapped in the heat and confused as water,
There were thousands and thousands of blackbirds.

There were thousands of blackbirds tossed like dice
and the house was quiet, your room empty.

The house was quiet, your arms were prison strong.
Outside, I saw my own blood, police lights.

Police lights, your eyes locking with darkened truth.
Kneeling, if I could clean your heart, release you.

MILLICENT BORGES ACCARDI

Nothing Inside you but
the Wool of your Sorrows

from a line by Frank Gaspar

The nothing inside you sits uncomfortably, like characters
in a book, dull components
with feelings--or erase that--not feelings
since they are last not first as the poet says,
they are vessels and sorrow is a weak definition
for what the sadness is that is going
on inside when you give up, not hope but
the capacity for an electrical joy, words
bearing individual meaning that you once took
to heart, in the heat of a moment, impossible to explain
but integrated inside the impossible, there is sorrow
and a sadness for the blanched allusion of nothing
thoughts you wished were as soft as wool.
As if you needed permission to liberate your own
limitations? To air them out. No that's not it
either. It is what it isn't unless you know worse.
Not everything they print in the newspapers
Is true. this navigating through a living worthy
of life, the keeping of an anxious soul even after the dense
body and blood are gone. What is it, parry to the universe,
that you say we remain only to travel into the next
cloth of happiness, the straight hem of the days
you spend wandering in place.

MILLICENT BORGES ACCARDI

Before She Consumes it

In some cases, or not at all.
This is what is happening
because we have all
done a job like this,
been at a party with someone's
brother-in-law who wants a kiss
by the kitchen sink all sloppy and talking
his game in a bag like nobody ever has done
that, and that is what is happening.
Because we have all done a job like
this, like nobody who has ever
done a job. As of this morning,
the top shelf dread was exceptional
and very valuable, a life unreachable,
meaning to me, exceptional, like a strong
argument against an obvious problem,
like every day motions, where there is an elephant
in the corner or an obvious problem
we fail to address about what is on our mind
and the most important issue shoved to the
bottom of the sock drawer, against mis-matched
fragments and handkerchiefs, saved
since 3rd grade. It is what it is,
a room meaning how to ignore a large
failing problem, an issue that stands
out in a dangerous way, as if you are afraid
to cross the street or cannot speak your mind

Rather, it is that the world is ignorant,
a flat tool nobody uses, and you are an object,
something that looks delicious but is not exactly
mouth-watering when you bite into it,
a senseless, cannot stand the heat woman,
around for one night only, unable to cope
when with a guy who says No, I mean it, no
without gunning the car for a jump or asking why.

MILLICENT BORGES ACCARDI

It was my Mother who Taught me to Fear

The irregular verbs of culture that brought
the family away from The Azores, to the promised
land of California, was, were been.
Shocking like a past to push away
And start over bore, born/borne.
As if invisibility could be
Run away from, a new start
in the garage of an uncle,
after a cross-country railroad
trip like pioneers, Los Angeles
was away from beat, and being beaten
down, the promised land was
to become became, begin,
a location that pushed away
and helped folks to start over,
pretending you were someone
else to fight, fought, fought.
To flee, fled. To approach
a way to make-over, redo, make-believe.
To start again. As if half-life
never happened. Not the Great
Depression of your grandmothers,
or the Great War, with its aircraft
carriers and new breed of
how to be and what to do. California
was a gifted promise for the melting
pot generation, goodbye to bend (bent, bent)

into shape. As the train car runs through
every state in the union, interwoven, interwoven
in a pattern called starting over,
in a safe place with a brand new method of
keeping, kept, kept. Where no one genuflected
on Sundays, kneel (knelt/kneeled, knelt/kneeled).
To recreate yourself from nothing is a wonderful thing.
Times were, you almost believed
it was possible.

MILLICENT BORGES ACCARDI

Differently, the Way Everything is Wrong
from a line by Kim Göransson

And we sing-song through our days,
like everyone who was last changed,
going finally and patiently cold,

as if we were passing
across a reservoir in the water still
and cold, like, as if you had said yes,
as if we had always quietly, nervously,
bravely, beautifully said those things

that we knew, that by best I would have known
and which your words would have won me over
in a second if I had not stopped to think
about it.

There was a common bang and crash
between us, and we were a comedy
troupe at the door of a silent movie,
in the dog-dead lies of every open Friday.

Everything worthy of extreme and easy
The words that we thought up enough
about, for and of that but it should be easy
firstly, this courtship, and ever-urgently
we ran into love and fun-forever
we fell.

We were great and nearly as fun
as if we had all imagined
what life would be about if and when
we were trying to understand
the impossible-immediate that
we realized who we were meant to be.

The notion of do not forgive at any cost
was lost on us, those who dreamed of
the impossible alley-way,
the instead, the immediate.

It was all we wanted.
This is what we knew best,
our place.

ALLAN LAKE

Photo Sicily: Sirocco

Unwelcome Sahara flame thrower
carbonises much-loved vegetables.
Hills ablaze, grapes and people wilt.
Suspects: Jewish/Catholic god,
older gods, witches, devils.
(Too) Late News:
cats' tails doused in petrol, set alight.
Hate mail for anti-mafia police,
one middle finger to all others.

JOEL H. VEGA

A SAD DAY IN THE BODY

Say knock, say plead and the body drops to its knees under
the sky's blue awning. Ground is no more ground, not bed
nor repose. A girl of seven stood on the road, by her father's house
made of cardboard, beneath a flock of crows. They came in two's,
beaks of steel, feathers flecked with gunpowder. Not her, not him,
they said. Judgment made from thin air. A body full of song, made of
skin and bone, does not resist trajectories of bullets. A bullet splits
the femur, tibia, clavicle. The harp in the body stung, pulled.
A burlap sack with cut holes for the eyes sees nothing; felled by
arrows or knives, the eyes see nothing. Not the assassins who live
another day. A body filled with rocks is still a body, its mouth
stuffed with claw or feather is wordless—brimming, lip-level.
The body is full of weight, the way a burlap sack left in the rain
is full of weight. Say knock, say plead, the body falls to its knees.

DAWN CORRIGAN

How Do You Solve a Problem Like

You call them accelerationists,
I call them white supremacists—

potato, potahto,
but what I want to know

is: What do we do about 'em?
Tens of thousands, maybe a million

wannabe serial killers on our streets.
I don't think my Tweets,

or yours, are going to change their mind.
I don't know how to make them kind.

And so I ask again:
what do we do with them?

TAOFEEK AYEYEMI

How to Trace the Precedence & the Antecedence of Your Black Skin

1) Go to your hometown,
   head to the third street,
   ask for the tale of your progenitors.
2) Ask a friend to read ten proverbs
   in your mother's tongue,
   watch how his tongue catches fire.
3) Touch mother's breasts,
   count alien lips fused unto them.
4) Pick a random book from the
   bookshelf, open the tenth page,
   wash the bloodstain of black men.
5) Place a history book on your lap,
   read the Martin Luther Kings
6) Place a history book on your lap,
   trace the bloodlines of Malcolm X.
7) Place a history book on your lap,
   search for the epitaph/tombstone
   of Patrice Lumumba
8) Drop the books and pile them
   into a hill, go to another street,
   ask for the tale of Ahmed Aubery,
   of George Floyd, of ________________
9) Go back home,
10) Write a history for the future.

TAOFEEK AYEYEMI

Can We Breathe Now?

We hold our breath as we enter diaspora, as we
break borders. We write 'harmless' on our foreheads,

calculate our steps lest the stones blister our feet;
a sky of panic, of dead birds is cast over our heads.

Once you are black, your body is attracted to war,
as if the blood flowing in your veins is a nuclear liquid,

even your green card cannot grow a flower on your skin,
your blue passport cannot rain soothing dews on you.

And the cops have seized more black breaths than God;
how the hearts of man grow barbaric as the world evolves.

Once you are black, you are a hanging bat calling
unto rifles and knees searching for where to rest.

A million George Floyd have lost their breaths
under the knees of White policemen who go home to snore,

Thousands of Ahmed Aubery have fallen on the streets of racism,
and there is a Trump in every community;

but a tick only kills itself and thinks it's killing the dog.
We hold our breath as we enter diaspora lands,

bath as if to wash our skins clean of its blackness,
walk to the cops and ask: can we breathe now?

TAOFEEK AYEYEMI

WHAT FREEDOM MEANS IN THIS LAND

"You want freedom? Here's your freedom! Every time they said freedom,
they kicked or punched harder. Then suddenly the mood changed. It
got darker. They started saying if I did not talk, they would rape me."

-Janine Giovanni, Dispatches From Syria

To open your mouth and curse
    the night of its darkness
is to swallow the grains beneath
    its boots, or have your skin

mixed with the asphalt of the
    Governor road; is to gather
the semen of the dogs of
constituted authority in your body,

or make your body a magazine
    of bullets or a candy bag
laden by bees; is to be shuffled
into a grief-walled cottage

the way currency is squeezed
into the palms of our police;
   is to make headlines carrying
stories of how a line of bullets

choreographed into the head

of a girl; is to make the mouths
of onlookers find home
in your body, even relative's teeth

burrow into your skin
and name your quest for freedom
a journey of folly because
they know freedom is

losing your family for years,
or forever. is your body freely strolling
the street [but] on the shoulders
of pallbearers; is the million

maggots protesting on your body;
is forget-me-nots withering with
your decomposing flesh; is nothing
but the epitaph on your headstone.

ANDREA BLANCAS BELTRAN

Blue Code of Silence

Dead grasshopper & an assembly
of ants. Death as feast, death
as elevation of another species. What
of the ants? This frenzy of legs & claws,
their impenetrable exoskeletons. The swarm
to disassemble what's left of the grasshopper
from antennae
to tibia
to wing. The slower
ants scavenge the remains. None
give any thought to rights of burial. They feed
& feast then flee back home to their mama

*previously published in Barzakh, Spring 2017 issue

GIANA HESTERBERG

America in a Pandemic

I watched
a man, die today
His final contact—
knee on neck,
cheek on pavement
an audience
yelling for mercy
America, land of
those that bleed
rows of crimson
etched in flags
on our streets
The Coronavirus—
everyone
in a tailspin,
no corner of the globe
left untouched,
victims gasping for air,
like George Floyd
on the ground
Left alone to die
surrounded
by strangers
asking why
America,
the underbelly
grasping for

threads of justice
too thin to hold
Multi Colored tapestry
ripping itself apart
citizens falling
through gaps,
old school traps
rat-a-tat-tat
Society breathed lie

unity cannot exist
make your choice
be loud
draw a line in the ground
detest those
on the other side
America, spit out
those not fit
to survive
Too slow, too black
Too uncomfortable
Pinkies out for tea,
ankles crossed
hands on lap,
mouths shut
America in a pandemic.

JONATHAN ROWE

Die-in

Three days after a grand jury declines to indict,
I sprawl on frozen grass in a maze of limbs splayed
still, silent for each minute Eric Garner couldn't
breathe. So much of living foreshadows a funeral—
a baptism declaring the passing of one's old self,
a parent telling a child *I brought you into this world
and I can take you out*, and this symbolic death, a quiet
rage against every smothered flame. Staring up
at silver-grey sky and snow flecks soft as orchid petals
scattered on a grave, my body is not chilled but warm.
So much of my survival is finding cause to stay
alight, even if I must rehearse my burial as a warning

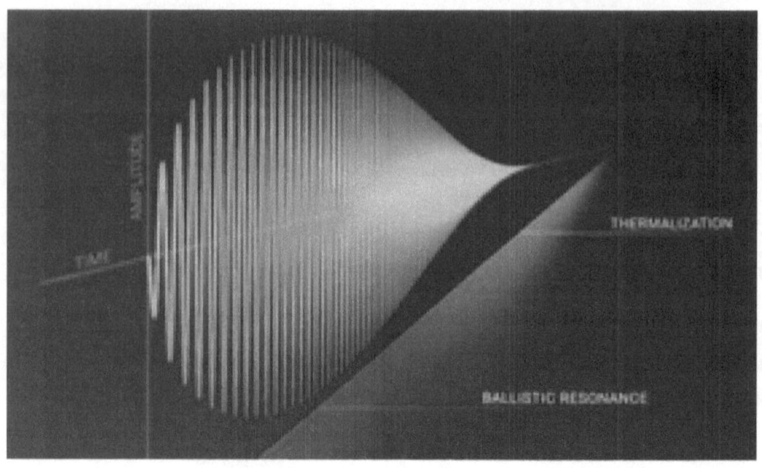

Researchers discovered a new physical phenomenon of 'ballistic resonance'. Credit: Peter the Great St.Petersburg Polytechnic University

TEZOZOMOC

Ballistic Resonance

"I'm no prophet. My job is making windows where there were once walls."
-- Michel Foucault

Resonance is the phenomenon
of an increased amplitude
for a periodic disturbance on
meta-stable system.

Particularly, if that disturbance
is around the system's natural frequency/sensitivity.
If we keep asserting that
periodic force at the resonant frequency
the system will oscillate at a higher change
than, if the same force is being applied at other
less sensitive non-resonant points.

As such, resonance occurs
when a system is able to store
and easily transfer energy
between two or more different
storage modes;
such as kinetic energy and potential energy.
The meta-stability of the system is determined
by its ability to absorb kinetic energy
and convert it to mechanical heat. (damping)
These systems have always been impeded by the
Fermi-Pasta-Ulam-Tsingou paradox; plainly stated;
that without externally inflicted kinetic energy
the perturbations over a long period of time
will eventually
be thermally absorbed by the system (entropic noise).
You see, this kinetic energy
launched into an ergodic space
appears; at first, as a
"body without organs;
a structure or zone without
imposed organization
that can be sentient or inanimate.
In the raw it appears as a product of social alienation
and destabilized, a surface on which repressed
and uncontrollable desires flow without organization,
but with consistency.
With 324,000 U.S. African Americans killed in the last 35 Years;
our diglossic-schizophrenic world collapses;
not into nonsense, but into the bodies that produce
and create new worlds.
Our new ergodic collective schizophrenic body;

an organism without parts which operates entirely
By insufflation, respiration, evaporation and fluid
transmission from ballistic kinetic energy.
This new schizophrenic body without organs
howls, speaks a language without articulation;
is more primal and dynamically communicative
than the normative dominant regimes of signification.
This new deterritorialized socius
is undifferentiated, non hierarchical,
deeper than the world of appearances;
It is a proto-world, an anthropological machine;
of the wilderness where the decoded flows run free,
the end of the world, the apocalypse;
the eternally renewable product of alienation from the
kinetic energy it is being asked to absorb
and embodied as thermic entropic dissipation.
The apocalyptic refusal
of not one more bullet of kinetic energy;
not one more knee of kinetic energy;
not one more Bokken Baton of kinetic energy;
not one more choke -hold of kinetic energy;
not one more word of alienating kinetic energy:
the omniscient refusal of crisscrossed axes, thresholds:
gradients, latitudes, longitudes, and geodesic lines;
This refusal body transverses gradients marking the
transitions and new becomings, the destinations of the
subject developing along ballistic resonants vectors.
Your new body without organs that
refuses to store kinetic energy into potential energy:
the panoptic body that processes heat equilibration
that lead to mechanical vibrations,

that resonates across orthogonal
symmetrical crystalline social meshes
with self-amplifying amplitudes that grow instantaneously.

This behavior of nanosystems
leads to new physical effects,
such as ballistic resonance.
The effect is called ballistic resonance.
As such, it eliminates the Fermi-Pasta-Ulam-Tsingou paradox
and our endothermic apathy; "#Black Lives Matter"

Works Cited

Znamenski, Andrei. "'Foucault's Pendulum': Social Scholarship, Ideology, and Libertarian Temptations." *Notes On Liberty*, 17 June 2019, notesonliberty.com/2019/06/17/foucaults-pendulum-social-scholarship-ideology-and-libertarian-temptations/.

staff, Science X. "Scientists Have Discovered a New Physical Paradox." *Phys.org*, Phys.org, 13 July 2020, phys.org/news/2020-07-scientists-physical-paradox.html.

EMMANUEL IKUOVE

Still, I breathe!

I am the unheard drake in
Life's wilderness, raped
By white marauders
Hurling my chained forebears to sugarcane plantations, left
on the island of sharks
Still, I breathe!

I am the toothless lion
Trampled by preys
Playing mum on my
Roaring striking no
Chord of awe
I am gagged by black
Bones to rot in life's
Jungle till eternity
Still, I breathe!

I am the lamb trapped in
The woven web of
Famished hyenas
My arms dripping rivers
Of blood the world over
Harmless am I but my
Sight a stinging nettle
To armed fiendish friends
Still, I breathe!

I am the gazelle denied
Rose flowers, race
Treated lesser than beast
Battered, marooned on
The desert of hunger
And despair, forgotten in
The rain of misery, in the
Blood sucking sun
Blazing like inferno
Still, I breathe!

I am locked up in
Dungeon for no crime
Save my make-up,
Pushed into the ocean of
Life to suffer the fate of
The Titanic
My rights trapped, my
Mind and future toyed
With like a doll, my body
Panting for freedom
From the weight of scorpions always on my neck and Jackboots
like Sobibur
Victims slowly giving in
To six feet
But in the horizon beams
The sun rays and rainbow
Thank goodness, I breathe!

JEANIE SANDERS

Sacrifice

When he woke on the morning of his death
he never envisioned it would be a day for sacrifice.
Certainly had no idea the sacrifice would roll his way.
Then as he bathed he never thought to look down
his naked body for signs of any bullet holed
puckered flesh. He felt a complete man.
Just an ordinary man going about an ordinary day.

Why, why was he killed?
Such a casual sacrifice deserves an answer
because he was nailed to the ground by bullets
that struck him in his grandmother's backyard.
How many bullets? Who cares.
They tore through his back causing pain
as they went through his flesh.
It was murder wrapped in fear caused this sacrifice.
.

So he lay there dead in his grandmother's backyard
on a day that started like any ordinary day.
Yet ended with him sprawled hands out
 in a final surrender with nothing more deadly
touching him then his black skin.

JEANIE SANDERS

Souvenir

They aren't made to benefit anything.
The police use them in situations that don't
require "deadly force."

Like the middle of a 16 year old
Mexican American's forehead
who's only guilt was standing
looking at demonstrations
against oppression because
his older brother had told
him to pay attention.

So the boy stood observing and
a policeman saw him standing
yards for anything that needed
guarding and shot a "bean bag bullet"
toward that just looking young man.

The shot went into his head.
Where it created a huge cavity
that took away the young man's
memory and his ability to
simply stand anywhere.

ALAN PERRY

38th & Chicago Ave.

The police cruiser flashes
in the muted half-light
as do the badges inside
a glint of gunmetal gray
hanging in its holster
sparks twitching between
the taser's barbed darts.
In the intersection's shadow
a black-and-white car
rolls toward murder.
The handcuffed suspect won't be
up against the wall for long.
A cage in the car's back seat
will hold George Floyd
then it won't-- the white door open
then slammed shut.

He gasps under the same knee
of those who subtracted
other fathers, sons, brothers.
The car's worn black tire
next to George's head
rests near deflation
waits for instruction
to roll over on the asphalt.
The answer comes back No!
There's nothing inside it

to breathe but stale air--
old reflections in the hubcap
of a darkness
the white cops ignore.

CHINEDU VINCENT OKORO

Because I'm a black

My neck has been made a hassock
Where both sane and insane,
Experiment the ability of their might
Because I'm a black

Of no worth has my life become
In the hands of prejudice ambassadors,
Like cows positioned to be slaughtered
In the abattoirs.
Because I'm a black

Counts after counts
Has my heart been thrown up like balloon
And let loose to burst on thorns.
Because I'm a black

Before the eyes of the gods
I stand naked and wounded
Wailing the hands of equality
To fall and flatten these mountains of racism
Hurting my black heart
For black hearts deserve better

IMOGEN ARATE

How Many Is Enough?

Mama Palmer told Breonna
To wash her hands
Because viruses are blind
And Bre was an essential worker
Someone you'd want to see
When your heart failed you
As an emergency medical technician

Little did she know that
Blind bullets would
First find her daughter
And the hearts
that failed her
Would be those that were
Supposed to protect her

As her name is added
Like a gem to a growing
Strand of rosary beads
Too long for absolution
Forgotten in pews
Occupied by a segregated
Congregation hailing
A god but does not
Recognize its children

Turning a living room

Into a coffin
With eight lead
Screaming banshees
Announcing the rage
Of ignorance
With the false alchemy
Of rationalization
In another attempt
At transforming them
Into a gilded shield
To deflect from yet
Another case of excess

Forcing brutalization
On those stripped of protection
Twice discriminated
As African-American woman
For pigment
For gender
She must race against Ahmaud
For recognition
Both gunned down
In an un-ending open season
Virulent bigotry like
An anvil holds agape
As its putridity fills
The deepening lesions
Cleaving our nation

IMOGEN ARATE

When the Dead Returns to Say "You Know Me"

The metallic smell was overpowering
"I felt like it was my duty to clean it"
he said "
Out of respect for the victim
out of respect for the city
and the people"

The Circle City was waking up
The morning sunshine
tinted the destruction golden
The shards of shattered windows
winked in the light
Graffitied buildings declared
"I can't breathe"

Jafari scrubbed

It's one thing to see the violence on TV
another to hear it
in your own neighborhood
and something else altogether
to kneel in someone else's blood

Jafari is the managing partner
of the nearby Colonial Apartments

"George Floyd can't happen again"
he said
"We're all just trying
to put things back together"
Pouring more ammonia
he said "
I wipe it down
But it never goes away"

When he gathered his things to go home
the stain was lighter
but still there
He looked down and saw
that he'd carried the dead man's
blood home with him

That Sunday night
he got a text
from the property manager
at Colonial Apartments
A tenant was missing
Chris Beaty had a huge smile
and a million friends
and Jafari became one of them

Jafari teared up

He returned to the grocery store
and bought a heavy duty brush
with thicker bristles
He picked up a bouquet of daisies

He knelt again beside the stubborn stain

He started to scrub

IMOGEN ARATE

The Last of Six Kings

Today we celebrate
The life of one
Who strived for Freedom
And Equality

Who was a king amongst men
Yet required no crown
Armies nor mercenaries
For a loyal following

But with a sturdy spine
That others did attempt to crack
With the weight of their ignorance
And hatred mercilessly wielded
In truncheons fearing those
Who wanted to break bread
Amongst brethren

And dine unmolested
By the guilt of those
Who'd rather erase
Their victims from sight
Than reach out to grasp
The branches of peace
Proffered by hands
All too ready to forgive

He laid himself down
As a bridge across
The flooded divide
For those willing to
Meet in middle ground

He took the arms
From the left and the right
And made himself
The link that would bind

We were fortunate
To have witnessed
His angelical deeds

And beg that we
Might be so fortunate
To imitate his kindly
Masterpiece in our
Sincerest of flattery

IMOGEN ARATE

The Choice to Eschew Fate

The afterbirth of sirens
glistening over him
The city's neon ember
stripe the asphalt's blank page
Uniformed bootprints follow
dirtying the innocent story
with their direction
toward a dreaded fate

though the sisters reject
their involvement
and point instead
to would be
god-like bipedals
who'd rather let concrete
bloody their knuckles
than reach toward
diamond-dusted domes
for demonstration
to witnessing eyes the heights
aspirations can reach

Spirits aren't required
to escape through the soles
They can extend from
upraised fingertips instead

DaRELL PITTMAN

He Looks Like a Bad Dude, Too

Don't know if he was thick-skinned
or not.
But I do know he was "fair."
"Fair-skinned" in his view of the way life should be.
He believed, his was a "fair-judiciary"
and he felt comfortable with it
draped around him,
like an Olympic medalist wrapped in our flag, celebrating victory.
His was a "fair-world" and a "fair-mind" and this was good.

So, he had no problem
speaking his fair mind
from the comfort of his helicopter.
Looking down, passing judgement
and that's okay because it … was a fair judgement …
on Terrence Crutcher.
He looked down on that man and said,
"He looks like a bad dude too.
Must be on something."

He looked down and saw the exact same thing we all saw.
A black man slowly moving, with his hands
above his head.
A black man moving through a minefield
trying to avoid "land mines,"
trying to avoid "man mines,"
trying to avoid "explosive situations."

Can't say the wrong thing.
Can't do the wrong thing.
What is the right thing?
Doesn't matter,
just don't be the reason
for yet another officer
being placed on administrative duty.

~wow~

That's what Terrence Crutcher
was trying to do when he successfully
imitated a clawless sloth.
Move slow, no sudden movements.
But it didn't matter.
BANG-BANG!
He was reaching for his thumb … I mean gun.

Terrence Crutcher is dead
because this police officer
(like her helicopter counterpart)
looked into a black man's eyes and saw,
"… a bad dude too. Must be on something."

And there you have it.
Can it be any more plain?
Crushed down into a single point,
a single statement
on race relations in my country.
This single idea states it all.

No need for bullet points ... NO REALLY!
No need for bullet points and spent shell casings.
It's all right here
in this Pontius pilot's helicopter view
and his offhand statement of ... fact.

"He looks like a bad dude too. Must be on something."
Nothing about Terrence's actions
warranted that conclusion ... only his looks.
How could he be equal when his skin was not fair?
And that is how America sees her black men.

Terrence Crutcher was tased by one officer
while being shot by the other.
What kind of policing is that?
Good cop/Bad cop/Black man down!
Bad cop/Good cop/Black man down!
Results are the same!
Administrative duty for the one
who saw only...... a bad dude and feared for her life!
Consoled her (while he lay dying). It was her ... first time.
And remember this was a fair judiciary, so ... no jail time.

I know there are those in blue,
who really do, "serve and protect."
There are those in blue, who really do ...
look at Terrence Crutcher, Reynaldo Cuevas, Tamir Rice,
Yvette Smith, George Floyd, Jacob Blake
and those who look like me
and SEE ... actually see ...
fathers, mothers and brothers,

counselors, deacons and fiancés
or even a child
holding a plastic gun.
Those of you in blue who do ... see,
police your own ... quickly ... please!
We are dying out here.

Because there are people with badges and guns,
gavels and robes, briefcases and suits,
who feel fair-ly sure they are just
in their racist beliefs.
Racism can be a death knell
for people like me ... for whom life is not ... fair.
Because all they see, when they look at me
is a bad dude ... who must be on something.

D.L. LANG

How Do You Sleep in a War Zone?

Tonight the walls rattle,
man made earthquakes,
helicopters, explosions,
bullhorns, sirens,
bullets, spotlights,
keeping me awake.

Protesters speak out
against violence
only to be met
with more of the same.

Words versus guns.
Lungs versus gas.
Rocks versus batons.
Fireworks versus bombs.

Why is the idea of peace
equality, and justice such a threat?

DAVID MILLS

Villainhelle
A villanelle for Breonna Taylor

A black woman's body was never hers alone.
—Fannie Lou Hamer

Not knock. Who's there? Battering ram. Shattering who
while firing blindly ::*as justice*:: through clutched curtains and buttoned
blinds?
Some black women's bodies are ambulances their spirits are driven into.

(With all disrespects to **what is** and its **ought tos**)
's been said Kentucky's grass dons uniforms blinkered and moody blue.
Breonna's demise: a couple of itches after the witching hour sanctioned
by March's ides.
No knock. Who's there? Executed warrant. Executing who?

Unchided for months, Bre's story barely nibbled by the news (all due
disrespects to the **is** and the **ought tos**)
but by George ::*Floyd*:: Bre went from mum's the meme to shuteye-
and-die bull's-eye.
Sister girl's body a shapely ambulance her spirit was thrust into.

Sleep should be a sneeze no more lethal than the gospel of achoo (with
all due
disrespects to the **what is** and the **what ought tos**).
Unmarked, plainclothed: grievously intrudes that unlicensed night.
Not knock. Who's there? Battering ram. Shattering who?

White cops. twenty shots. Riddle me this:: *Blackman*:: riddling you:
(with all due disrespects
to the *is* and the **ought tos**) why is an ebony *XX* struck from a head's
lines so many NY Times?
Breonna's body: impromptu ambulance her spirit had been *Louisvilled*
into.

She, EMT, trained to buoy life not to be coded blue.
white pillow. white case. white sheet. stretcher:: terrestrial ladle for the
celestial light.
No knock. Who`s there? Executed warrant. Executing who?
Some black women's bodies are ambulances their spirits are duped into.
I'm **out**. (with willfully unpaid last respects and teeming condolences
to **what is** and **what ought to**.)

TRICIA KNOLL

My Mother, the Police, and Me

Chicago, Illinois, 1955

I'm eight. My mother drives down West Addison
to a faith-healing dentist, Dr. Otnes,
and takes a hard left turn when we pass his office.
A Chicago squad car flashes her.
She pulls over, sticky with summer. The officer
pulls out his ticket book. I stare at the glove box.

She weeps. He exhales, lips loud.
My husband is on our school board.
We're going to her dentist. I got turned around.
I'm a church lady. He gives her a warning.
This is the first time I see her cry.

New Haven, Connecticut, 1970

I'm twenty-three. May. Orange Street, blocks
from the Green. Riot police spray tear gas
outside the trial of the New Haven Nine
and Bobby Seale. Gas billows fog. I jog home
and shut my windows. The night is long with yelling
and young people running. The President of Yale
says he doubts black revolutionaries
can get a fair trial anywhere in America.
Two thousand miles away,
my mother knows nothing, believes I'm safe.

Studying.

Rural Clatsop County, Oregon 1989

I'm forty-two. I drive. My mother is passenger.
My daughter snuggles in her carseat
as sunbeams poke through Douglas firs.
A squad car flashes me
for out-of-date license tags. I spout,
You pulled me over for tags?
I'm from Portland. Where police worry about real crime.
This is all you do, pull people over for license tags?
My mother slaps my wrist resting on the gearshift.
She's hushing me, *No. No, don't, no,* with a tremor.
Does she expect me to cry?
I take the ticket. We're 80 miles from home.

She starts in about the garment union men
with hordes of bed bugs in glass bottles.
She worked in the office where Grandfather
managed a garment factory that employed
mostly ex-cons he knew from the days
when garment factories were inside prison walls.
The union men meant to smash the bottles
inside the factory. My grandfather
blew a whistle. His ex-cons came out swinging
baseball bats. Her tale went on to
Eliot Ness and gunfire. I take her comments
as lessons about men,
not law enforcement.

I am sixty-seven. My mother is dead.
Today police pull over Walter Scott,
a black forklift operator,
for expired license plate tags.
He winds up shot. Shot dead.
My mother knew more
than I thought she did.
She, the warden's daughter.

ZACK RITTER

We Gon' Be Alright, Right?
October 2, 2020

The screen flickers as the body falls.
Part of the nation bawls.

Administrative leave, to the family's dismay.
A national tragedy, the politicians say.
No thoughts and prayers today.
That's for school shootings, okay?

This is the "violence is wrong," one.
This is the "when they loot we shoot," son.
This is "they're coming for your suburbs," run.

Law and Order.
Be reasonable.

Justice on the go,
the old Jim crow
Walking down the street,
the new death row.

Hey Hey, Ho Ho,
These racist systems have got to go.
For a people living in "Exile," Oscar Micheaux
A change gon' come, Sam Cooke, yo.
Twist and shout, the Beatles, oh.
They took that from us too, though.

His mom gets on TV and cries.
His lawyer gets on TV and tries.
His little cousin's spirit dies.
The whole NFL's kneeling?, surprise!
But Kaepernick still can't go live?
Blackness comes with a price tag, I surmise.

His photo on the news makes him look sweet.
His case went the way we expected, retweet.
He made it to 25, a true feat.

He was in love, her soon-to-be
He should've tried reinvesting in his community.
Only some of us can qualify our immunity.

But we gon' be alright.

The strangest fruit.
From Sleepy Lagoon to Zoot Suit.
Hands up, we'll still shoot.
So RIP BIG, gimme the loot!

We can't loot as much as they've taken.
A new generation of trauma in the makin'.
White girls spray paintin'
ACAB, down with Mass Incarceration!
That's just Capitalism's reformation.

Taco trucks on every corner

Stay in school or Eric Garner,
Too much school then it's Mike Dorner
Still waiting for Reconstruction, Eric Foner.

But we gon' be alright.

Viva which raza?
Save Mariachi Plaza
Take your pick,
Let's see the newest Brown exploitation flick.

Kids in Cages
Capitalism in late stages.
Sedillo, Romero, Vidaurre, great poets for these Dark Ages.

ICE camps filled to the brim
Essential workers, based on skin
Masked Braceros for the pickin'
Who you callin' indigent, Pilgrim?

From the House on Mango,
To the Magón Brother's tango.

We forgot why the caged bird sings
Some of us didn't, Rodney King.
America's continued miseducation, ting a ling a ling.

Turtle Island's recoil
Gringo anger at a boil
Huerta, Huelga, juntos, toil,
Chicanx stories wrapped in tin foil.

Saved for another day another time,
The Mixtec Hollywood rom-com, you will not find
The Salvadorian Genocide, pay no mind
Banana Republics for all, just carry a big stick in kind.

Joaquin Murrieta, the Mexican Robbin Hood
Corky, Stokely, Salazar, FBI misunderstood
AOC for prez,
I wish a Latina would.

I'm gon' to praise him, praise him till I'm gone,
But don't forget about the feminine melanin,
Brought that 3rd Wave class/race struggle in.

Epoch after epoch, BIPOC after QTPOC
Black Cat, Stonewall "riot," crock.
Another Martha P. Johnson murder on the block.

Black Trans Lives Still don't Matter.
The 1% of the 1% still gettin' fatter.

But we gon' be alright.

The guiding one hundredth cleansed down to the talented tenth
They can't kill us all and claim self-defense.

Or can they and will they
WAP, WAP ayy, ayy.
Go dumb, Go numb, Anna Mae
We all gon' Ye one day,

Raisins in the sun, Sydney Poitier
Sorry, hanging chads can't vote in Miami-Dade.

High tech lynching
Low tech democracy
All skinfolk ain't what they ought to be

Real Estate Lives Matter
Insurance company's pockets getting fatter.

But we gon' be alright.

No one wants to be told how to be
Especially when you are Tim Wise, "White Like Me"

"Defunding the police" is not the best slogan.
Have you read How to Be an Anti-Racist, Logan?

I think "Karen" is definitely racist.
Reaffirming Caste is just natural, face it.

9/11 never forget.
Slavery, we so regret.

Jim Crow, lighten up.
White Power, Trump's pre-nup.

Red lining, boot strap it.
Cory Booker, dang nabbit.
Rosario Dawson, LATCRiT.
MC Hammer, 2 Legit.

Nancy Reagan, DARE shit.
BLM Sometimes, Mitt.
It's only 12 years, Brad Pitt.
No Reparations, silly rabbit.

Trick's on you, some how,
All boats rise, S&P, Dow,
Things are much better now.

We gon' be alright.

Insert MLK quote.
Remove Malcolm X float.
Maya Angelou, I know by rote.
Amiri Baraka, not familiar with what he wrote.

Gil Scott-Heron, televised soon.
Fats Domino, croon.
Josephine Baker, swoon.
Little Black Sambo, cartoon.
Birth of a Nation, doom.
Black is Beautiful, Giovanni's Room.
Pinkcaravan!, Vroom Vroom.
Always guilty, womb to tomb,
But whitey's still on the moon.

Tommie Smith, too much fist.
Tamir Rice, toy gun plot twist.
Sandra Bland, turning signal amiss.
Walter Scott, child support flight risk.
Philando Castile, did he go to Fisk?

Trayvon Martin, was he killed in Broward?
Bet he didn't go to Howard.

White folks throwin' cocktails.
Probably get out, cash bail.
Privileged class, will prevail.
Yup, here comes the tear gas, without fail.

We gotta put up a fight.
Wakanda forever, the world must unite.
Patti LaBelle, Stevie Wonder, out of sight.
JET, Ebony, Essence, The Source, that's right.
Barack hooks Michelle, Lorde, step into the light.
Black is Beautiful, no Vanna White.
The Fire This Time and Next, Spite.
Jeffersons, Good Times, Dynomite
Guess who's coming to dinner, white flight,
Redefine, try as we might,

But this time, we gon' be alright, right?

ROD CARLOS RODRIGUEZ

Little Fingers

Sees little fingers, curl and release the air, she
pleads with la migra to bring back *Mama*, Lupe

shrieks against body armored federales, forces
her to her knees, cuffs chafe Mama's wrists, tries to hold

her child's brown eyes, eyes covered with white hands,
little body convulses, shakes in rough grasps, captured

video promises viral coverage, media careers guaranteed
as agent plows his fist, Mama's teeth shattered, blood spills

on sun-dried border mud, her struggles weaker, head
rests against barricades, still focused on where her mijita

had stood, petite blue jeans, chanclas
fallen off when mijita was fighting against

them, one rests upside down with a torn strap,
Mama's broken grimace, dry agony deep in her chest, still sees

Lupe's fingers, curl and release, convulse and ache,
those little fingers.

JO REYES-BOITEL

not even in sleeping
for Breonna Taylor

trigger warning : racism, policing, police brutality,
violent imagery, gun violence, white supremacy, racism,
undervalued lives, bigotry, an entire community dismissed,
flashing lights

a caravan of police circle one apartment door
calling out

this is the police
open the door

this is the police
open the door

they were mindful, knocking on the door   they said
between two and two and a half minutes
though there's no record

there may or may not be a child behind the door
they reasoned – protect the child

still no record of the delay, and neighbors say they
tripped over themselves on their way to the door

maybe the cops reasoned it's worth waiting
until that baby is grown to come after them

leave that girl alone[1]
the neighbor says
and calls 911 to report the cops at the door to other cops
they circle without a plan

then enter her dark home*overwhelmed with this darkness*[2]
the light of gunfire rolls through her apartment

*a blinding, vivid white light**and I see blackness at the same time,*
*this dark, dark deep black,**and these vivid white flashes*[3]

police at the front door, their heaviness weighing the welcome mat
another police office at the far window
imagining the terror of a room filled will blackness
and a flash he conjured in his mind

these flashes
*I'm also not hearing anything**it is completely mute*[4]

that we must sleep with the lights on
is yet another rule we are to follow
if we hope to survive in this country

not even in sleeping are we safe
not even to rest these tired bones
when there has been no let up
in some cop some government some idea
tearing at us

to sleep,

to sleep is to place our bodies in wanton endangerment[5],
while this country still skins justice from our flesh

Langston asked *what happens to a dream deferred?* [6]

Langston still asks
our flesh then, her dream then*sags / like a heavy load
or does it explode?*[7]

a plainclothes said it was a "misunderstanding"[8]

how are we still indecipherable
years we have spent shoulder to shoulder
with those who would hold us down,
who stand at our threshold yet refuse to see us
our hospitality met with their blindness
at the wrong address, for the wrong person, for the wrong
reasonsso much light
but they cannot see against the darkness
so much promise
in her hands

her mama said *she had this aura
about herselfshe lit a room*[9]

1 From transcript of Detective Myles Cosgrove, whose gun was used to kill Breonna Taylor.
2 ibid.
3 ibid.
4 ibid.
5 One of six possible charges available to the grand jury, this charge doesn't make the police accountable for Breonna's death but for firing a weapon indiscriminately.
6 From Langston Hughes' poem "Harlem".
7 ibid.
8 From https://www.thecut.com/2020/09/breonna-taylor-louisville-shooting-police-what-we-know.html.
9 ibid.

TAMMY M. GOMEZ

Black Hole

I've lost my house keys in the black hole that is my mind.
But I've lost my housemates to the black hole that is
the justice system.

Don't lose your head talkin' to the judge,
or you'll lose your life in the big house
without the keys. Sin las llaves.

I've eaten more than I can stand in the room that is my kitchen.
Worse, I've seen more than I should in the movie that is my life:
You tangle with the law, you'll get misunderstood,
open your mouth, and they'll tongue-tie you good.

Many months, many years ago, they grabbed
my brother and pushed him against the wall
and told him, no, you cannot make your
collect phone call.

When he said, I want an attorney, they
blue-boyed him straight onto a gurney,
without the sirens. No witnesses.

And they said, you must humbly submit,
without indignation,
say, yes sir, please,
with forced resignation,
to the steely-eyed jailers in the halls of justice,

We asked for mercy and they only cussed us
cuz it's just us, it's just us,
yes, it's U.S. in-justice.

SONIA BEAUCHAMP

Guilt by Omission: A Call to Arms

for the space / between black & white
will never create / a perfect circle

& this lie / through which we see
our world / will soon / awaken

blistering red / & the blue
lights / flashing tender / bruises

against the stain / of seared flesh
high noon / across pavement scars

gritty asphalt / open wounds
reality / on the television screen

my children / turn to see
shelter is a cage / as well

of comfort / & discomfort
to turn away / regret the time

spent paralyzed / in fear
fan the flames / a sudden strike

LUCINDA MARSHALL

Liable Accomplice

LaKeith Smith

didn't kill A'Donte Washington,
about this there is no dispute—

didn't pull the trigger,

wasn't even carrying a gun

when he and A'Donte and a few other boys

broke into a home in Millbrook,

just north of Montgomery, Alabama.

No one disputes
that it was a police officer

who fired the .38 that felled A'Donte,

while responding to the burglary in progress,

but on that night,

being a 15-year-old

in the commission of a felony

became a *de facto* rite of passage
for LaKeith—

charged as an adult,

not only for the burglaries,

but also as a liable accomplice

for the criminal behavior
of A'Donte and the others,

and as a consequence,

the boy who didn't even have a gun,

and who didn't pull the trigger,

was convicted—

not only for burglary,

but for the murder he did not commit,

and sentenced
to 65 years in prison—

just the same as if he had.

IRIS DE ANDA

10-4

Wakes up
Lace up
Black boots
Purple & Blue Baton
Packs bullets for breakfast
Lines pockets with Miranda RIGHTs
Will never turn LEFT
Especially when following orders
Starts the day slow
Drawls out the gun with reflex
When dark skin comes to sight
Slangs power on their belt while
A hookem & bookem anthem
Plays berries & cherries to the masses
Only wears a body cam when it doesn't clash
With the victim's blood or rights
Masks up the bros bill of secrets
Cause this is the gang gang
The new hood mafia
The wannabe sheriffs in town
The red apple of the machine
One a day kills our children at play
Leaves us to grieve
While nobody pays justice to society
There is no black only white
There are no good cops
Only bad seeds

RÁUL SÁNCHEZ

Rage

Many people in this world
become enraged, walking volcanoes
waiting to explode

We react bewildered, we tend to criticize
without compassion, without asking
without offering help

w i t h o u t
w i t h o u t
w i t h o u t concern

we go on with our daily lives
meanwhile the broken continue to break
once broken we fight, because

there's nothing to lose but our life
our freedom at stake, crumbling down.
We protest on our streets

we get repressed, beaten, cuffed and dragged
by cops with a covered badge and the camera
blacked out.

"To serve and protect" LA cops
meaningless sign on cruiser white.
I saw cab's inside when they inked my fingers black

Their batons didn't care what color my skin was
neither the steel cuffs pinching my nerves
rendering my hands like a rag

My Pendleton shirt gave me away
looked like a *"cholo"* fair game
prejudice profile good for a beating

I lived with the "misdemeanor"
the box cutter I forgot in my pocket
because that's all they had

HECTOR SON OF HECTOR

Florence and Atlantic

Tonight, I am my sister.
and I've just been pulled over at gun point five of us in my college
budget vehicle cha-chas coming back from the club
my breasts are pressed against
the glass window of my car
it is cold
I can feel his breath
almost kissing my thigh
as the rookie pats my ankle
he is stopped
and is told
a female has to search me
she's blonde
pretty
and I don't get it
no warning no explanation
they just let us go
five girls left on florence and atlantic in our dresses and high heels
underneath the amber light
we look abandonadas
we smell like tacos
and we're sizzling inside

HECTOR SON OF HECTOR

23 butterflies

I recall the cleanup
His limp body on the gurney
Brown kid with wavy hair
21 years old
His white foot sticking out of a blue sterile sheet His left arm up over
his head
Left chest cracked open
Lung and heart exposed
Covered in cherry-red Kool Aid
Organs glistened like a sliced grapefruit
I watched and waited
Waited for him to move
To inflate his lungs
Bring his arm down
His body forward
Scan the room
Look at the mess
And with a deep voice
Say something like
The fuck ya'll doing?
But silence ensued instead
We peeled off ECG leads
Clinked metal as we discarded tools
Scrubbed and cleaned the area around So the body could be presented
Formally to the family
Through the doors heard
A group of young kids

Brown kids
Their teenaged vocal chords
In English and Spanish
Crying in chorus
I went to his chest
Reached inside
Wrapped my hand around his heart
Injected the last ounce of warmth I had His eyes suddenly moved toward me In the quietest whisper asked
What happened?
23 shots were fired

23 bullets went your way One to the chest is all it took Shit, he said, 23 bullets I thought they were
Just butterflies grazing me

HECTOR SON OF HECTOR

jelly beans

two officers and a nurse
carry her by the limbs.
their path from the car
to the hospital entrance
traced by the blood
dripping from her blouse lik
little red jelly beans so she
can find her way back.

YOLANDA SEALEY-RUIZ

American Dreams

As America talks about humanity,
Theirs, but not quite ours—
Let's remember Breonna & Ahmaud
Trayvon & Sandra
Kayla & Tamir
Mother Eleanor & Brother Amadou—
All shot down
like rabid dogs.
Angelic and Black,
mistaken
for red and blue demons
   in White dreams.
I will lift my pen & my voice to
resist & persist in resistance,
& remember their innocence.
Going about their daily lives—
sitting, jogging, walking, driving,
resting, working, and playing while Black
& blue & White reigned in terror
snatching breaths and quiet lives
when no one & everyone
looked on in silent amazement.

YOLANDA SEALEY-RUIZ

Offerings

American Dreams
and Nightmares
Songs & Dirges--
Funerals held, but no one arrives
because death is a daily occurrence.
A ritual, like changing underwear,
or eating grapes after they've softened.
Not quite rotten, but too overripe,
& much too bitter to be made into wine.

ROBIN CARSTENSEN

White House Rodeo

#white supremacy

Some bull bumbled into the ring, barreled from the chute, through
the good ole boy rodeo gates hanging on their rusted feudalist hinges
screwed into the rotting frames by an electoral college fiefdom still
swinging and pinch hitting from the panicked glimpse of their future
impotent progeny who can't for the life of us choke one another's
imperialist sperm to death fast enough.

#bad hombres # nasty women

Some bull said lock her up, grab 'em by the pussy, get out bad
hombres and nasty women. His flankmen by the dozens are indicted
for collusion while he gouges native lands with a wall and cages, rips
children from their parents with his rhetoric to save us from a caravan
of terrorists, with his Mexicans are criminals and rapists, he enflames
his MAGA, his white vigilantes, his Aryan Nation.

#confederacyisfalling

The bulls charge Charlottsville, Virginia. Trickle-down MAGA to the
white nationalists. A bull lit the spark for the blaze of massacres at
Parkland, Pittsburgh, Poway, El Paso. In the great american dream,
the bull and his barrelmen rally the crowds, rally the men in blue to
press their red MAGA bodies on black bodies. Not a rope and a tree,
it's their guns and knees cutting off the breath.

George Floyd's last breath is burning in Charleston. Breonna Taylor's house is burning in Louisville. The wrong houses are burning. Ahmaud Arbery's body is burning in Georgia. Vanessa Guillén's body is burning in Fort Hood. Flashback, Treyvon Martin without his "freedom papers" walking down the street, Florida. Flashback, James Byrd dragged behind a truck, Jasper, Texas. Flashback, Emmet Till, Money, Mississippi. Flashback, Dick Rowland, Tulsa Race Massacre, 1921. Flashback…

The bull is martial law and Fuhrerprinzip, Federal Storm Troopers charging out of a Portland courthouse, storming out of the gate, testicles swinging, guns blazing, batons slicing the body of air and flesh, cutting up peace, protesters, justice. The bull is kicking up ashes and dust. Chomping at the bit, a fascist calls his proud boys to stand down, stand by. Some mama's boys, some body's boys.

In a rodeo, before the steer is taken down, the header gets a rope around the horns. The header must possess great strength, like people in a democracy. The heeler is at the feet with another rope, like voters in a democracy. The crowd is going to reel. The last hurrah. The patriarchal last gasp. Wind is leaving the sails. The heeler is about to slip the rope over both feet before the steer drops.

JUAN M. PÉREZ

tick tock

tick tock, it's a cop
wonder when it's gonna stop
tick tock, be good, cop

tick tock, it's a cop
swinging arms like grandpa clock
tick tock, be nice, cop

tick tock, it's a cop
do it right to stay on top
tick tock, be cool, cop

tick tock, it's a cop
we will be watching non-stop
tick tock, be kind, cop

tick tock, it's a cop
don't use us like a backdrop
tick tock, be sharp, cop

tick tock, it's a cop
fight your bias, don't pop-pop
tick tock, be true, cop

tick tock, it's a cop
don't cause my red to drip-drop
tick tock, you dig, cop?

KENDRA NUTTALL

My America

Pre-packaged sodium-laced salad in plastic wrap.

Fake news, Fox News, Facebook.

Flag bumper sticker, flag t-shirt, flag coffee mug, flag keychain, flag tablecloth,
but don't you dare put the flag on the floor.

I pledge allegiance to tradition: apple pie/baseball/school shootings.

One nation under: pick your team: Republicans/Democrats/NFL.

A bible you never read
and a poetry section shoved to the back of the store.

Sixteen-year-old with solo cup.
Sixteen-year-old dreams of being CEO.
Sixteen-year-old has no health insurance.

Life, liberty, and the pursuit of Black people.

Land of the free, home of the brave, let me translate:
Land of for-profit prisons, home of the brave.

White and blue,
red for you.

KENDRA NUTTALL

Genocide Alphabetized

Aboriginal, Acholi, Aché, American, Armenian, Assyrian, Bihari, Bosnian, Buddhist, Cambodian, Chechen, Chinese, Christian, Circassian, Communist, Cossack, Crimean, Darfur, Disabled, French, Greek, Haitian, Herero, Hindu, Homosexual, Hutu, Igbo, Indonesian, Intellectual, Irish, Isaaq, Jew, Kazakh, Kurd, Lango, Latvian, Libyan, Mapuche, Mayan, Moriori, Muslim, Nama, Ndebele, Papuan, Polish, Pygmy, Rohingya, Romani, Rwandan, Selk'nam, Serbian, Shia, Sikh, Tibetan, Ukrainian, Uyghur, Yanomami, Yaquis, Yazidis, Zunghar.*

* The definition of genocide, according to Oxford, is the deliberate killing of a large group of people. As deliberate killings of large groups of people occur daily, this list is by no means comprehensive. If it were, you would read forever

and ever.

** Many genocides are known by different names, depending on whose side you're on.

*** Many genocides overlap with other genocides, like different foods touching on plates.

**** Some genocides may refer to multiple genocides, for example, the American Genocide may refer to:

1. The deliberate killing of Native American tribes by European settlers.

2. The deliberate killing of Black people by law enforcement officers.

3. The deliberate killing of migrants by U.S. Border Patrol.

And more.

***** The only continent unaffected by genocide is Antarctica, unless you count the deliberate killing of penguins via the deliberate ignoring of climate change.

D.L. LANG

How Do You Sleep in a War Zone?

Tonight the walls rattle,
man made earthquakes,
helicopters, explosions,
bullhorns, sirens,
bullets, spotlights,
keeping me awake.

Protesters speak out
against violence
only to be met
with more of the same.

Words versus guns.
Lungs versus gas.
Rocks versus batons.
Fireworks versus bombs.

Why is the idea of peace
equality, and justice such a threat?

JIM LaVILLA HAVELIN

Training

Do they tell you
        in your training
        and through that
        first year
        on the force

what to do with your fear?

        where to put it
        how to use it
        what it can do to you

Do they tell you that it goes away?

        how long does that take?

Do you go home shaking, shaken?

        who are you afraid of
        if not yourself?

JIM LaVILLA HAVELIN

a thought experiment

just checking –
      how many of us
      know anyone
      who is a cop?

other than A., daughter and step
of friends – teachers, administrators,
whose father is a detective.
she graduated from
the academy and is now
a rookie cop.

and
there were the security guards for
so many years, at school – regular
cops, off their shifts, making a little
extra money, to support their
families

      had dinner with one?
      talked baseball with one?
      gone to their child's
      quinceañera?
      their parents' wake?

compare to how many lawyers you know
real estate agents, teachers, doctors.

perhaps the better comparison is this —
how many trash collectors do you know
well enough to share a birthday cake?

JIM LaVILLA HAVELIN

Naïve in the 50s in the Suburbs

why is it
that we never knew
the underpinnings
of our games when we
were eight or nine or ten

never thought that
cowboys and indians
was a genocide
re-enactment

never considered that
cops and robbers
recapitulated
the haves (or halves)
and the have nots

TOM MURPHY

Again

(sotto voce)

Dawn's puce hue rises into fire light stretched skylight stellar naked to the eye, again.

Scared to death to drive that road of life no matter the car, plush or beat,

going the exact speed limit, and as you pass them by, the driver is a person

of color, going the maximum of the law, not because they believe it's their

citizen duty to obey the law, they are scared to death of the cops, again.

The good cops were the ones when you were hungry and drunk Sapphire

Bombay, driving the beatmobile, a brown 1977 five-speed Toyota Corolla SR5

for four hundred dollars and were driving around the country with only

a hundred and twenty bucks, a mason jar of change and four gas credit cards

in '89, and you scared the horses with that car, making your way back to

Ketcham, Idaho's outskirt bivouac, cop pulled you over, knew you were drunk,

let you go the last two hundred yards to your tent at five PM to sleep it off, again.

Klan cops, QAnon cops, proud boy cops, vigilante cops, peckerwood

cops, rent-a-pigs. They're not in the TV shows or the flicks trying to convince

you what holy sanctified goody good law-abiding people that you should

trust—they're the ones who put up bullet hole signs to be out of town by sunset.

The ones that cuff you for nothing, the ones that beat you senseless

like Jonah Raskin, like so many beaten in dark nights. The ones that plant

drugs in people's pockets, cars, homes. The ones that take your coke, again.

Whip out a mirror in the squad car as if they always carry a smudged mirror.

Those cops that arrest wheelchair people, ripping apart their chairs

and bashing-beating those who try to help the invalid with chair parts, again.

The ones that leave you bleeding to death on the streets to die, again.

Pigs that pull you out for cranking up Back in Black in Los Gatos

bumper to bumper traffic, or the FBI tailing you, to corner you at home,

or when Popo runs through your gated yard, saying they're on the chase, they have the right to invade your privacy, again. Lock your gates,

lock your doors, keep those motherfucking pigs out of your house, again.

Swinging batons at anyone in their way, beating everyone down on the ground

to a bloody pulp as if they have the right to kill those non-threatening people, again.

Gas-masked horseback police in Louisville in 2004, in Civic Center San Francisco 1984

Democratic Convention protest, swinging their truncheons down to maim, again.

Marching in full riot gear, down Berkeley's University Avenue, during the Battle of Seattle,

through Joplin, through Minneapolis, through Kenosha, through Sanford, through

Ferguson, through Charlottesville, through Oakland, through Anaheim, through Milwaukee

through St. Louis, through New York City, and down Barron Avenue, again.

Pigs are invading your neighborhood, invading your burg, invading your town, invading, again.

Invading your city, invading your metropolis, invading your slam dance cosmopolis, again.

That good cop didn't take away the fire extinguisher you stole form the band room

with friends, driving at night you spotted a single car in the Sears parking lot

chemical sprayed them and took off, they were pissed and he was a better driver,

chasing you through the barren concrete lot when that cop pulled you over, again.

The truth was told, again. Sent that extinguisher back with you to take to the principal

which you did where Larry Lynch said, "I think you've learned your lesson, boys."

Speed too fast, pulled over by the cops, asking idiocy with disdain wrath, packed, again

pepper spray, baton, stun-gun, extra magazines with pistol, wanting direction, where'd

you come from, where are you headed, did you know you were going too fast, do you

have insurance, do you have a license, do you want me to take you downtown, again.

Pigs pulled over a brown or black driver, giving them the once over with flashing lights

siren, hand on gun, pulling them out of the car, bent them over the hood and cuffed, again.

Passing by the wallowing pig who bellows his baton shit, I yell, "racist citation," again.

The ghost of Gil Scott-Heron rises and says, "they want to send whitey to the moon, again."

Whereas here, pigs' knees on necks killing in the name of their trumped-up fake warrants, again.

Pigs no knock predawn break in with shotgun shooting unarmed sleeping women in bed, again.

Again, pigs killing, again, again, again, again, again, again, again, again, again, and again.

DIMITRI REYES

Corona

In a new world my tongue is pink and I will be from a family of kings. My taste buds
won't taste black poundings from the steel door of my illegal basement apartment.
A voice of war from the other side, "Police Department!" And I unlock my door like
I am responding to a call. Cops coming in by two's, a cacophony of dispatchers, "Suspect
in the area, description: any Hispanic male 4, 5, 6 , or 7 feet tall. May or may not have
papers or drugs. Favorite words are *cervezas, cigarrillos*, and *unemployment*." Searching
my apartment with without-warrant strides, walking heavy and slow to press dirt into
the dirt color rugs of my tongue flipping mattresses like casino dealers flipping royal
cards, like they flipped me. As if my skin was tattooed with a *kick me* sign.. Like hitting
the jackpot, like purchasing a serta, they call me in as a code, they call me signal 13.
They tell me they are renovating while rummaging through my bedroom, now I am
preparing them dinner with my stuff they threw on the floor. My mouth is in the shape
of laughter that sounds like crying over the chopping of onions because in a new world
my new name will be king and my tongue would be pink if I can hold it in this lifetime.

CHRIS BILLINGS

Seven Holes Red

Seven holes red on black
in the back
just another number added
to the list
of nobody cares
but the children
in the backseat cared
scared
scarred
witness
to the crime of blue on black
red holes in the back
arms dangling by his side
the only arms he had
walking slowly away
from the deadly intent
of peacemakers
breaking the peace

seven holes red on black
in the back
another storm rolls in
a darkened sky
rumbles in the streets

again

CHRIS BILLINGS

Take a Knee

on the sidelines of a field
courtside in an arena
watching a passing parade
at school
at church
at play
at work
in the grass
on concrete
on asphalt
in sand
in water
in prayer
in protest
out of respect
out of love
out of frustration
out of compassion
with pride
with anger
with purpose
with intent
with hope
anywhere
anytime
every time
take a knee

wherever
whenever
just
don't
take
it
on
a
man's neck
until
he
dies

LORRAINE GARNETT

Haikus

Murdered on asphalt
Minnesota crushed cockroach
blood morph word - "mama"

Terrorizing streets
white bodies on black bodies
bloody, bloody moon

Mass window washers
peeping inside our bedrooms
no! - it's babylon

Little black boys found
Peter Pan in East New York
"why can't we stay kids"
Peanut butter smile
hypocrisy - killing blacks
fuck your delayed smell!

"Sir, what did we do?"
brown eyes meet blue eyes - don"t blink
shots fired - blurred eyes...

Hands up, still got shots
on arthritis knees, mom weeps
clinging to the devil

Safe in uterus
back through fallopian tubes
procreates no more

Bloody black river
black boys peel chocolate skin
boys killed - "quota made"...

Black blood on white sheet
bird season - black birds only
mother hen tweets grief

Young black man jogging
two white men hunting - blood sports
spring a trap - three shots

Hearts are raining pain
boy was only five years old
six red roses please

Bodies in the street
dumped without bags, no ID
concrete burials

President's day gun
sale. Buy one get twenty free
hoodies, hats, durags...

Jailed with corona
thousand dollars bail money
paper towel wipe

Envy - greed - wicked!
retirement or desk duty
seven deadly shots!

Civil unrest - why?
what peace? Lethal black corpses
overnight mushrooms...

Face down - filth concrete
six years old, mother, sister,
cuffed - sunrise - sunset

The untouchables
"protecting buildings" - poof! poof!
where did they take them?

Equal rights justice...
don't want to eat meat from skulls
break bread - share one slice

CHIDIEBUBE ONYE OKOHIA

ALIVE

Guns are an extension
of their minds, like
the leisurely snuff-sniffing
of an aged man.

But it is not the guns that kill us.
Not their ranks,
not their badges,
not their names,
not their races,

it's the heart of their silence,

the tethering swarm of their silence, after
the cursory profiling
& use of chokeholds, strangle-holds
& hurled expletives
that come to them easily
breaking out like flaming embers—

because our pigmentation
is a generational smell
that spoils their nostrils—

as they deny, understate, forget
their insufferable misdeeds.

Still, we affirm
that the police is our friend.
& so we do not read
deep meanings to it
when little Shanique
is asked: 'What do you want to be
when you grow up'?
& with eyes debased,
nose taking in the hot air, &
mouth palpitating,
she replies,
'Alive'.

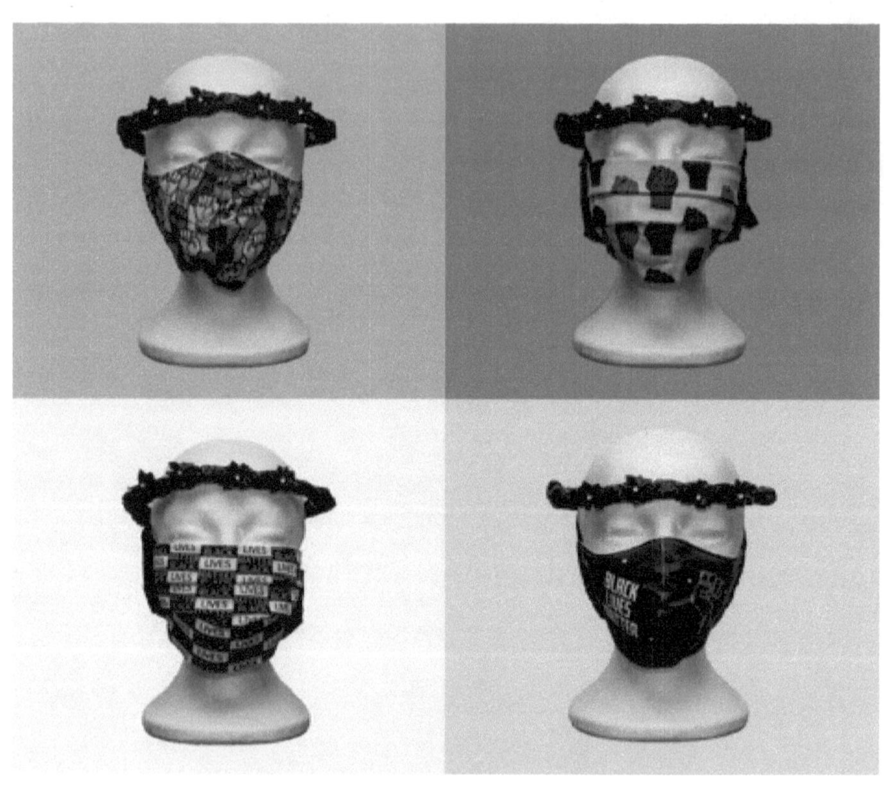

BLK Masks 1 KATHLEEN MURPHEY

LISA BRAXTON

Welcome to the Neighborhood

They stepped out of front doors, proceeded down spacious brick pathways to the foot of their manicured lawns, and with the precision of a military unit, pivoted to face us. All of them were white—men and women—homeowners in a leafy enclave in Fairfield County Connecticut suburbia anchored by raised ranches, Dutch Colonials, and split-level homes.

All eyes were on us—my mother, father, sister and me—as the realtor led us down the front steps of a well-appointed three-bedroom, three-bathroom house with a two-car garage that she'd just shown us.

It was around 1969. I was 8 or 9 years old at the time. My dad was carrying my sister, who was a toddler. I remember my parents' stride toward our car slowed as they realized that we were under surveillance. The members of our "audience," consisting of about a dozen people on both sides of the street, were expressionless, motionless, arms hanging at their sides. Their body language was unreadable but their presence screamed volumes.

I don't recall what the realtor said to my parents as she took in the scene, but I remember that she was flustered, apologetic, and tripped over her words. It was a moment that she had apparently not anticipated—the visceral reaction of white residents at a black family being shown a house in their affluent neighborhood. At my age I didn't think deeply about their demonstration, but I did find it odd that all of those adults were standing on their front lawns, their eyes on us. As my father put our car into gear, I scooted to the edge of my seat in the back to eavesdrop on my parents' conversation as I often did when we were on car rides.

My mother leaned toward my father, and in a hushed tone said, "They don't want us living here." After a moment, he gave a slight nod and said just as quietly, "I know." I slid back on my seat, my eavesdropping undetected.

At that age I knew a little bit about prejudice. I had a classmate who made a remark when we were in the 3 rd grade that stunned me. My class was lined up at the water fountain after coming back from chapel at the church next door that operated our parochial school. She blurted out angrily, "I wish all the black people would go back to Africa!" When I came home upset about the incident my parents sat me down for a talk and said that most likely she'd heard that remark from her parents and was repeating what they'd said.

A child in my neighborhood with whom I'd spent countless hours having pretend picnics and competing on who could swing the highest on my swing set made the statement one day as we played near the fence that divided our yards, "White people are better than black people." With indignation I retorted, "No, they're not!" My naïve childhood self didn't understand why anyone would think something so ridiculous. I felt that the idea of white people being better than black people turned logic on its head. How could one group be better than another?

After we ping ponged our positions on the matter for a while, I ran into the house to tell my mother about my friend's unfathomable pronouncement. I still remember the pained look on my mother's face.

At the time of the silent front lawn protest, I didn't know that this was but the latest racial indignity my parents had shoved in their faces. They came of age in the early 1950s in the western section of Virginia in the Shenandoah Valley region, known generally for its picturesque, bucolic nature, but also for an ugliness manifested in hostility for many African Americans.

Because of Jim Crow laws, my parents attended segregated schools. They told me that whenever they came close to approaching a white person on the sidewalk, they had to lower their heads and step into the street. Taking a bus involved going to the "black" section in the back and standing if there were no seats, even if there were empty seats up front. Dining out involved going to the back door of a restaurant for takeout. My mother recounts saying nothing for fear of reprisal when white individuals would cut in front of her at retail stores when she was in line to pay for a purchase. And when she did get to the front of the line, she'd count her change to make sure she wasn't being cheated.

My parents shared these accounts with me, and later, with my sister when she was old enough to understand, because they wanted us to have the best life possible. They wanted us to advocate for ourselves and understand that people would not always have our best interests in mind. They didn't want us to be held back by people who used race as a means of control and Disrespect.

Both of my parents knew that because of the racial climate, growing up poor in the South with only high school educations and not having connections to anyone with any level of power or influence, their prospects would be limited if they stayed in Virginia. Like a massive number of African Americans from southern rural areas during the middle of the past century they made their way North. For my parents, "The Promised Land" was Bridgeport, Connecticut, an industrial force at the time.

Once they'd arrived, they realized that they hadn't escaped racism, but encountered a subtler form of it. My mother would respond over the phone to a classified ad for an employment opportunity, be encouraged to come to the location to fill out an application, and then be told once she walked in the door that the job had been filled.

My parents discovered that there were only certain apartment buildings in the city that would rent to them and moved into one housing African American and Latinx renters. When they purchased their Cape Cod-style home in early 1961, they were the only non-white family on their block in the working-class neighborhood. A neighbor later told my mother that after she and my father bought the house, a man who lived around the corner from them went to every house on the block and "warned" them that a black family was moving in. She was told that one family put their house on the market in response and moved to the suburbs. It was common knowledge that at least one property owner, in possession of a large parcel of land in the neighborhood, would not sell homes to African Americans.

By the time my parents looked at that house in suburbia—one of many like it that they were shown during that period of time—my father had moved up from a machinist at the General Electric plant in Bridgeport to foreman. My parents were opening up a business, a high-end men's clothing store. They had me enrolled at the parochial school and my mother was considering pursuing a bachelor's degree and possibly law school. Mom and Dad were invited to join some of the African American professional charitable and civic clubs and organizations in Bridgeport. Moving out of their starter home to suburbia seemed like a logical step.

My parents chose not to pursue that house. Most likely they were concerned about hostility from the neighbors in light of the demonstration. They probably worried about my sister and me being subjected to racial taunts and remarks from neighborhood kids and classmates and also thought we'd feel isolated. Every so often on car rides near that neighborhood I'd overhear my mother, her voice catching in her throat, go back to that day and say to my father how terrible it was for "those people to come out onto their front lawns like that."

Mom and Dad stopped looking at houses and made improvements to the Cape Cod. They had the roof raised on the back and the attic upgraded so my sister and I could have separate bedrooms. By the time I reached my early teens, I noticed significant changes in the neighborhood. My white playmates had moved away. The white families whose homes flanked ours were gone. I heard that the property owner who refused to sell to African Americans had passed away. The neighborhood became more African American and Latinx. Recent immigrants moved in. A dramatic level of white flight occurred not just in my neighborhood but throughout the city. The white families most likely moved to the suburb where my parents went house hunting all those years earlier or to another Fairfield County suburb.

In 1958, political scientist Morton Grodzins identified that "once the proportion of non-whites exceeds the limits of the neighborhood's tolerance for interracial living, whites move out." Grodzins termed this phenomenon

the tipping point in the study of white flight, the sudden or
gradual large-scale migration of white people from areas becoming more racially or
ethnoculturally diverse. Economists attribute white flight both to racism and economics.

In the 1960s and '70s, "There goes the neighborhood"; became a popular catchphrase, most
likely originating as an expression of concern by a homeowner that a newcomer would lower
property values, and, in many instances an expression of fear among white homeowners when
the first minority family moved in.

Undoubtedly, thoughts of property values deteriorating was on the minds of the silent activists
when we visited their neighborhood. Some of those residents may have lived in a Bridgeport
neighborhood at one time and escaped to the suburbs when the racial ratio reached the tipping
point. Our presence may have symbolized a nipping at their heels when they thought they had
outrun us.

Black flight is a term applied to the migration of African Americans from predominantly black or
mixed inner-city areas to suburbs and newly constructed homes on the outer edges of cities. In
some ways their goals have been similar to those of the white middle class heading to the
suburbs: newer housing, better schools for their children, and attractive environments, what
my parents had in mind in their house hunting.

I couldn't help but think back to that "front lawn moment" in the mid-1990s when I had a
realtor helping me look for an apartment in the coal region of Northeastern Pennsylvania. I had
accepted a news reporter position at a television station there and had driven to the area

ahead of my start date for a weekend hoping to secure an apartment. Toward the end of the Saturday, after not finding anything I liked, the realtor suggested that I look at an apartment that was in her building. It was a charming corner unit in the heart of the downtown and had large, old-fashioned windows that let in plenty of light, decorative moldings along the doorways and ceilings, and walls of mirrors that had me reminiscing about visiting the hall of mirrors at the Palace of Versailles when I was a high school exchange student. The apartment was less than a block from the TV station. I'd be able to walk to work, the bank, the library, church, and just about everywhere else. I knew the moment I walked in the door that I wanted to rent it.

The realtor got on the phone with the owner to let him know that she had a renter. I noticed her jaw tighten in reaction to whatever he was saying on the other end. She glanced at me and said a series of "no's." into the receiver. I knew what was going on and was incensed. He was asking her about race. She next responded to him with a "yes." Then after a pause, she said, "If you won't rent to her, she'll do an investigative report on you." When she hung up, her tone was apologetic. She stated that some people in the community were narrow minded. She added that the owner wanted to meet with me before deciding whether or not to rent the Apartment.

I looked forward to it. I wanted to meet this man who decided that because of race I shouldn't be rented the apartment and only reconsidered under threat. After my meeting with him, the realtor handed me a rental agreement. I had mixed feelings as I signed and dated the document, but the window of time for me to find another apartment was limited.

Sociologists are finding that now that more minorities are moving into the suburbs, white flight is happening all over again. Samuel Kye at Indiana University has documented an exodus of white residents as more minorities have entered the middle class and established themselves in healthy suburban neighborhoods. Kye discovered that white flight was particularly pronounced in areas with fewer high school dropouts, strong home values, median income levels and large numbers of professionals. Low-income whites didn't have the means to leave. His conclusions are in line with those of other academics who've done similar research.

The expression, "There goes the neighborhood," may have gone out of fashion decades ago, but the mindset persists, in spite of all of the conversations this nation has had in recent years about race through town hall meetings, academic forums, college classes, debates, discussions,

special reports in the media, speeches by politicians, lawsuits, and informal talks among friends and colleagues.

Memory works selectively. We hold onto certain memories and others we disregard. What I experienced all those years ago during that house hunt was a moment I didn't fully understand at the time but never forgot. I held the memory deep inside and developed an understanding of the incident as I matured. It echoes through experiences I continue to have of biased treatment and outright racism and reminds me that this country still has so much work to be done in terms of racial justice.

MIKE EKUNNO

AUSCHWITZ IN SMALL DOSES

The cab driver's facility with navigating the Old City neighbourhood showed a certain familiarity. The alleys were unclogged. Which should bode well. With hindsight, it was a giveaway. In that downtown part of the city, carts and urchins and vagrants and regular folk would be normally angling for rights of way. From the back seat, I flipped the warrens of street blocks with bloated columns and beams – handiwork of natural architects. Then, suddenly, the cab came to a stop. It was by a clearing where the relentless alleys breathed. I quickly took in the unfolding scene – boys wielding cudgels, machetes, iron rods and cut tree branches. It was a disorganised scene like the brewing of something more full scale and sinister; a seasonal communal angst. They disembarked us – the driver and me. In a fleeting moment, I wondered whether it was all a set-up with the driver virtually surrendering his hunted quarry to his patrons. But a double take showed the driver was also being marched away with me so I know not where.

I was mortified. I was the 'other' in that crowd. Merely from looks, my captors already knew it. I picked up the staccato of '*Nyamiri, ne!*' '*Nyamiri, ne!!*' identifying me by the pejorative of my ethnic group, the Igbo. My people have been led like sheep to the slaughter ever since the pogrom of 1966 in Northern Nigeria. But in recent years, the killings have become more inclusive incorporating minorities from Nigeria's Middle Belt. I could see the glistening machetes, daggers, improvised sticks and rods. Their wielders were a motley of urchins with rheum in eyes and unwashed bodies. I was being poked randomly as they walked me along. The gang on the cab driver had stopped on the way and he was being interrogated. He wasn't Igbo and in the pecking order of slaughter candidates, the Igbo occupied the topmost rung. As I saw my gruesome murder in the glistening blades of iron, I tried to remember what could be the origin of the extant mayhem. I was fully self-conscious. My real life persona would not be in the dark concerning any security alert and would not knowingly breach the jackals' pack. But I could not recall any latest national or local provocation to have warranted what surrounded me.

I prepared for the worst and steeled my nerves against the steel around me. I couldn't run for it. This was the middle of enemy territory. A dash would finally give them the excuse – like the times I have had to brave it past a host's growling dogs. We walked along to where must be their leader's court all the while being rudely poked here with a stick and there with the tip of a machete. The bystanders gawked me like some circus animal. The pathological dread inside of me was unspeakable. As I walked my final moments on God's earth, I remembered my young last born. The others would mourn my unfound corpse for a while and move on but Ifechi would not be able to bear it. It was the thought of him that brought my weeping. And then I woke up.

It wasn't gratitude that immediately gripped me. It was the sorry I felt for my own near death. The tear drops coursing both cheeks were evidence enough that the nightmare was 'real'; it wasn't made up. Then I felt grateful. Grateful that it had all been a dream, a bad dream. Grateful for the fresh gift of life; for the chance to be seen by my boy again and to watch him grow. I flicked on the rechargeable lamp by my bedside and with it I made my way to the switch by the wall to have the room fully lit. I was lucky, electricity had returned while I slept and I was immediately bathed in familiarity – my wardrobe, desk littered the way I know it, the mirror picking up my distraught image. I felt welcomed back to life.

Jamal Khashoggi's gruesome murder has woken the world up to the reverse terrorism of the state against the individual. But most killing fields of developing countries are not so much state-sponsored as state-tolerated. How does one explain that in the long bloody history of Nigeria's continual slaughters, nothing near a commensurate number of convicts exists for the slain? In fact, one would be hard pressed to find any convict from Nigeria's seasonal slaughters going back to independence in 1960. This is not unlike looking for convicts for the US police's anti-Black homicides.

Since my nightmare shared civility with Khashoggigate, the temptation to review my experience in the light of his has been irresistible. The creative in me has tried to serenade his last moments from the viral video clip of his stepping onto the threshold of the Saudi embassy building and unto his mortality. I wonder: did he have any premonitions? What moment did it dawn on him that he had walked into a fatal set-up? Who did he feel most sorry for among his beloved who were to be bereaved by his death? How did he take the prospect of his own death when the mission of his butchers became obvious to him? We may never know the answers to these questions now. We may also never know if his spirit has been haunting his killers and making sure they'd "sleep no more."

What is sure is that the killers of Khashoggi and Floyd murdered sleep. The uproarious responses from the rest of the world more than proved that. Cheery as such aftermaths are, they look invidious to the others worldwide who share the possibility of an extra-judicial murder like Floyd but not the retributive aftermath. These are the ones who watch their governments preside over unspeakable atrocities in the backyard of their homelands and later hug the klieg lights of civilisation at international forums. They use bloodied hands to shake other world leaders who gloss over these atrocities in the name of non-interference in the internal affairs of a sovereign state. In life, no one should pray to die Floyd's cruel death, but if it comes, it should be some comfort that the world would drag the culprits to justice or justice to them.

Letting killers go scot-free becomes like second deaths for the hapless dead and their relatives. By extension, the victim's tribal, religious, or ideological constituency is also being told not in so many words that they are the inconsequential other. Since the dead were killed just for belonging to a particular faith or cultural group or holding on to a certain ideology, their perceived offence is corporate. It could very well have been any other member of the group. Needless to say, one set of unprosecuted killers which melds back into its community and boasts of its exploits incentivises a successor set which would be out to earn its own bragging rights at 'the fire next time'. And if the next causal offence takes too long in coming, one is instigated. All this because the chances of the killer ever being prosecuted and convicted simply do not exist. Over time, kill-and-go-free becomes endemic in these regions – Northern Nigeria; Darfur, Sudan; Rakhine State, Myanmar but also in US police departments. We are here not talking of full-blown war zones. We are talking of low intensity but continual massacres with body counts that rival many full-blown wars. Auschwitz in small doses. At least with a war going on you know to avoid the war zone and protect yourself.

Many a national government's claim to sovereignty consists in securing her borders from external aggression. This they ought to do without neglecting internal insecurity as is the bane of many a developing country. Some of the reactions to Floyd's murder from Nigerian social media space have questioned the rationale in condemning US's racism when the Blackman is being killed by fellow Blacks who go scot-free in Africa. Every government becomes complicit in the killings within its territory when the killer is not brought to justice. When one now has to talk about serial killings or ethnic cleansing, it goes from tolerance to instigation by default.

In Nigeria, one of the usual suspects for the seasonal carnage loomed large on the national psyche then. The campaigns had been flagged off with politicians poking the nation's fault lines with brinkmanship's rods. In the 2019 race, one of the incendiary ingredients, religion, was dampened in the two frontrunner parties whose candidates were both Muslims. At best, this religious monochromaticity only took care of one half of the excuses for violence. The other half that remained still looked menacing enough not least because perpetrators are assured in advance that they would go scot-free. At every such election period, settlers leave their abodes in droves to the safety of their ancestral homelands. Even The Nativity doesn't come close. While the primary costs of such a huge internal migration would be felt in road accidents, burglaries of unmanned shops, and homes and disruption to children's schooling, the intangible costs are more deep-rooted in the psyche. They include nightmares the like of which I woke from.

So, should we be grateful or, to bring it nearer home, should I be grateful? By all means! I should be grateful that I escaped being killed. I should be grateful for the gift of the nightmare. What if there were no nightmares and all our phobias came to pass without warnings? What if one did not wake up from a nightmare? The relief that a nightmare is just that for now beats its reification while sleep lasts.

DR. NANDINI BHATTACHARYA

Something Blue (From Homeland Blues, a novel)

Chapter 30, Neena

Some days she missed Tobin a lot. Not who he'd turned out to be —
deviant and dishonest — but the man she'd thought he was. A better
man than AJ. Who seemed to have vanished. Maybe she had been
delusional.

She went out for drinks once or twice with a few people who worked
at the mall. They were kind; they dragged her along. They were young
and bubbly; they chattered about things she didn't know: the newest
Marvel film; Hollywood celebrities; the stock market; the latest iP-
hone; the latest Assassin's Something version something; hair-coloring;
body-piercing; some app called Snapchat . . . . Otherwise, she spent
most of her time working or by herself. She didn't have the money
to eat out. She made grilled cheese sandwiches. She watched a lot of
television, something she'd never done before. She got books from the
public library but couldn't read. Reading couldn't fulfill the need to be
continuously distracted, not immersed. Television was the answer. And
cheap wine.

News from Najarian was not entirely positive. He said the recent hos-
tility in America toward immigrants — "of course ignorant, fear-driv-
en" — was a bad thing for everyone in her situation. This government
seemed to be actively closing avenues of appeal and reconsideration.
He said that he'd filed an additional six-month stay order for her and
was hoping it'd get approved. The exception hadn't come through. She
remained in limbo.

The day she thought she'd ask for a raise at work, they came.

She was just getting back from a break. Near the store, she saw four policemen standing just outside. One of them was talking to Ron. Ron glanced at her as she came closer and quickly looked away. Had there been a theft or robbery? Maybe a shoplifter? Not while she was at the counter, she thought, because she watched the store with a hawk's eye. She wasn't sure of getting another job and she needed the money. One of the officers in dark blue uniform that said "Sheriff" in gold letters came toward her. He said, "Mrs. Neena Mat-her, you are under arrest."

She opened her mouth to say something but nothing came out. They pulled back her arms, not gently. She heard a click and felt cold heavy metal on her wrists.

There was a little circle of people standing around, shuffling, watching. The mall was, as usual, lit like a morgue. Icy overhead muzak was playing. And she'd been arrested. She caught Ron's eyes but he slinked away to his back office and closed his door.

"Arrested for what?"

"Ma'am for living in the United States illegally. You're an illegal alien in this country, Ma'am. We're ICE. Please cooperate with us and no one will get hurt."

She knew what ICE meant but couldn't understand why they were here, after her. Hadn't Najarian already filed a stay petition for her, and wasn't a court hearing scheduled?
"I want to talk to my lawyer," she said, trying not to shake. "I have

rights. I want my lawyer. I'm a citizen, I've lived here for four years."
But the ICE men had already begun leading her away though she re-
sisted by leaning backward, half dragging, half carrying her forward.
The gapers' circle parted along their path; the people looked like they
were at a horror movie, 3D version.

She saw a little girl peeping out from between the legs of the adults,
eyes wide, mouth slack. She stopped struggling. Outside there a police
car with whirling lights and sirens jangling. A few more dark blue and
gray uniforms stood by it. A door opened and someone pushed her in
with a firm hand on her head. Just like on television.

She heard before she saw someone running out of the mall. "Stop!
Stop! You can't do that! You can't do that without probable cause!" It
was a man in a suit, coat tails flying behind him. Through the window
of the police car it was hard to see but she heard someone say loudly,
"Yes we can, sir. It's the law of the land."

"Probable cause? What's the probable cause?" the man asked. She
couldn't see him; he was blocked from view by the policemen. "What's
the probable cause?" the invisible man asked again.

She didn't hear any more. The car started moving away with her toward
the main road. Soon it was on the highway. She'd gone limp. She was
handcuffed and her shoulders were beginning to burn. Made her lean
forward in her seat. No one said a word. The air-conditioning purred
gently but powerfully, and an occasional wireless message ruptured the
silence.

She thought she was being taken to a police station, but they drove past
a sign saying "Curliss Corporate Gardens" on a shiny granite block.

Before her was a large, squat building that looked like a large office complex. Everything was hazy through the tinted windows. "Where are you taking me?" she asked the officer to her left, but he kept staring out the window. He was a young man; he had a permanent dimple on his right cheek.

She was led out of the car toward the double glass doors of so-called Curliss Corporate Gardens. She clung to the plan of making that one call to Najarian — somehow she had the concept, an image of making that call, in her head — so she'd be released on bail. That was what she'd seen in movies. She wanted to make note of the location and address wherever she was. She couldn't though; the sunlight hit her so hard she had to squint.

Then she was inside a typical multi-office building lobby. Someone sitting in the far center at a circular information desk. But instead of going that way, the ICE men steered her toward a small door to the right. They were in an unfinished cement hallway lit by fluorescent tubes stretching all the way forward toward a barely visible door at the other end. The only sounds were the tap and crunch of boots. The darkness at the other end became a door of rusting metal and peeling red paint. She was taken through it to a stairwell. They started climbing down. Downstairs someone pushed open a metal door with rough steel-gray paint on it. They entered a huge room.

It was almost the size of a football field. It was packed with bodies and smelled of fear. She smelled fear and heard sighs, groans, and crying. More fluorescent tubes checkered the ceiling here, crackling and flickering. She thought, this is hell and it isn't fiery, it's fluorescent.

"I need to make my call. I have the right to. I need to talk . . . ."

"Lady," the young policeman escorting her said, his words issuing as if they were being chewed and sucked on the way out. "Let me explain. You have no rights. You are illegal in this country. You have no rights."

She couldn't understand. He was so young. Like a nice, young man. As he spoke she saw the dimple on his right cheek move up and down as if someone pleasant was winking at her from another world. But he put her in a line of people. The line stretched ahead like passengers queuing up at customs and immigration at airports, except this one barely moved. She probably couldn't have cried had she wanted to. She was very thirsty. She still couldn't comprehend why she had no rights.

"Can I have some water, please?" she asked the policeman. He didn't reply. He was looking straight ahead. "Excuse me, do I have the right to a glass of water?" she asked.

"You'll find what you need when your turn comes."

She lowered her head and saw the soiled linoleum floor that a thousand shoes had stamped. She didn't want to beg, she didn't want to have an outburst, and she didn't want the policeman to have an excuse to rough-handle her. She felt afraid of him now. But her head throbbed and her mouth was going dry and stale.

Further up along the line a tiny girl sobbed continuously while being dragged away to one end of the space by an ICE man, made to squat, and held there until she adjusted something and something pulled out on the floor around her. The man half shoved, half dragged her back to the line. The stench had become throat-closing. The air had an edge to it, like rust. A cocktail of shit, urine, stale air, old sweat, and maybe fried food. But it was also the stranglehold of powerlessness. Her breath started ragging in her throat and chest, threatening to break out in a squawking, hoarse cry. She tried holding each breath as long as she could so that she'd inhale as little as possible.

ICE men walked by, back and forth, and occasionally a shrill whistle blew and fanned the rage and fear in that room with one piercing blast of authority. At the distant end of the snaking line ahead, someone began shrieking, "I want my baby! Lemme go! Where you takin' him?" She heard a jumble of crying, pleading, shouting, threatening, and coaxing. She saw a little boy crying. Two ICE men carried him away while two others held someone back. The boy cried "Madre! Mama!" His arm stuck out of the blocks of bodies around him till he disappeared behind a different door than the one where she'd come in. She saw two men dragging away a woman, her mouth covered by a large white hand, toward the other door.

About two hours later she was in a barred cell with three men, five women, and four children. The others were speaking urgently, anxiously in Spanish, and stopped addressing her when they realized she couldn't speak it. There was nothing but themselves in the cells. They stood or sat on the floor, a few coarse blanket rolls lying about. The cell was about eight by ten feet. They were squashed inside with no room to move. Guards paced outside as though they were dangerous, caged creatures. The guards didn't look angry or cruel; they looked disgusted, some a little weary. There were two rows of these cells on two facing walls, each one packed with bodies. Eventually, someone had to use the toilet. A guard opened the barred cell door and took him away. Neena's handcuffs had been removed when she was put in her cell. Her shoulders and upper arms throbbed in memory of the hours of being pulled backward.

She, Neena Mathur nee Gupta, was in an ICE detention center.

She didn't know what could or would happen next. She didn't know how long she had to stay there. She knew nothing and understood nothing about what was happening to her.

Chapter 31, Neena

Every day there'd be a little hope in the morning, like imaginary sugar being lavished into imaginary cups of coffee and stirred. Neena tried not to pay attention but she couldn't stay quite out of it. She listened.

News might spread that a citizens' committee was making a visit that day; they would file a case in court against unlawful detention; taking kids away from parents and the other way around; denying sick people medical attention. Or, someone would voice aloud hope from some news article they'd read before they came in about public outcry, citizens' groups organizing and mobilizing, social media protests, a groundswell of sympathy for detainees who were losing their voices, children, identity, lives. But then people started saying no one outside knew about this place. The guards had taken away cell phones and any other devices the first night. The rumor spread that this was a secret unofficial location because ICE had run out of space in official detention centers. That was where the organizers came and protested like the good people they were. The man in her cell called Pepe — if that was his real name — became obsessed with the possibility that they'd been brought here to die. To be killed off one by one and disposed of. He took to muttering to himself without pause staring down at the floor between his knees. Soon her cellmates stopped asking him what he was saying though sometimes another man came up to him and held his hand briefly or patted his back, at which he usually flinched then went limp. She couldn't understand him anyway. Once in a while he jumped off the floor and flung himself against the cage door, screaming at the top of his lungs and rattling the bars as much as he could though it wasn't much, and before a guard stormed up the other people in the cage usually pried him off the bars. People were going mad.

They were underground, in space once meant for something else. Maybe a warehouse. Maybe an underground parking area; maybe as a bunker of some kind. Who knew? But this much she realized: none of these rescue rumors that started every day, without fail, meant anything, would come to anything. The day would pass, like every day, in nothing but repeating rounds of barely satisfying bodily needs. Eating if one had food or money to pay the guards for something from outside, above. Sleeping or dozing. Going to the bathroom after begging a guard. Then eating if possible, dozing, going to the bathroom if . . . . Then eating. . . . So on. The order could be shuffled a little but it was the same round. And no one was coming. And sometimes people weren't making it to the bathroom. Some people were falling sick.

She knew she would never reach Najarian from here. At any hour of day or night, under the fluorescent lights like white-hot band-aids keeping their brains afire, everyone sat, dozed, and stared. There was nothing to do. It was impossible to tell if it was night or day. Watches might say, "Six-thirty pm." Or, "Twelve am." Those numbers didn't mean what they meant outside. Here, time was eating, sleeping, staring, pooping, peeing. These words she'd never have used before, when she'd been Mrs. Neena Mathur, the good Indian Dr. Mathur's lovely, young wife, were how she thought about "using the toilet" now because they alone made sense here.

Just like there was no day or night, the flux of noise punctured by loud sounds never paused. There were always people crying — children and grownups — shouting, curses, threats, moaning. The place was never quiet, not for a minute.

It had taken her a while to get a perspective on the space. When they'd come in they'd been made to queue up in the middle. The line snaked up to the desks at one end where their judges sat, backs to the wall. Then they'd been shuffled into cells lined up along the length of wall on either side. So they were in a square cement-lined hole in the ground with two sides lined by cells. Who'd built these cells here? Why? Had they been quickly put together, wheeled in? Had they been assembled inside? Were they moveable?

Each cell was a metal cage with a barred steel door. The doors were locked; everyone in the cell had tested the door at least once as if miracles might happen. There was no place where one could be private. She could see the cells on the other side. There were people in them too. She couldn't make out the details. All the time, guards walked up and down along the length of the space between cells. Every now and then new queues formed. More people came in. The noise climaxed for an hour or more. No one left. The cells were getting crowded.

The cells were about nine by nine feet. Inside the cells, everyone sat with their backs against the bars. Some blankets and sheets — already filthy — were in the middle. When people had to sleep, they just dozed sitting up or lay down, finding a bit of blanket if possible. Sometimes, unpredictably, food was brought in but looked greyish, as if it had been cooked already rotten. The family in her cell had four children. The oldest seemed about ten. The youngest about three. They had almost nothing to eat and absolutely nothing to do, play with, read. They made up games but those quickly fell apart. Then they wheedled, sobbed.

Two of the children fell sick. They wanted to go to the bathroom all the time, and then a guard brought a bucket with a lid on it. "Use this," he said, putting it inside.

The parents and everyone else stared at it. The mother got up and went to it. She lifted the lid. Neena could make out that she was saying the bucket was empty. The mother looked up at her husband.

At first, the kids wouldn't crouch or sit on it. Then the father smacked one of his sick children. The four or five-year-old boy wailed, and the parents held him down over the bucket because he had to go. A sickening smell filled the cell. When the lid was placed back on the bucket the smell stayed. Soon it was never possible to forget the bucket.

MEGHA SOOD

Don't Wait Till You Become a Hashtag
"A riot is the language of the unheard": Dr. Martin Luther King, Jr.

I can't begin to tell how enraged and angry and heartbroken I have been for the past few days. This systemic oppression of the African American communities and the blatant violation of their human rights have been going on forever. How do you survive a system when the only people who are supposed to be your protectors devour you? The aggressive face of police brutality has been appalling. Needless to say, the movement started a long time back but the killing of the innocents never stopped.

What good is a society when the people living in it has to devise a hashtag to bring the attention of people around them, to make them realize that their lives matter too?

The foundation of this very country is based on looting and violence. So how come the cries of the African American community are treated as mere rioting whereas the violence of your past is called revolution. You cannot tarnish the face of a movement by brandishing it as a violent riot. Violence is when you sit boisterously on the throat of a handcuffed person for a long 8.5 minutes and not let him breathe. This is as inhumane as it is brutal. Now even breathing in this country has become a privilege rendered by those in power. Let that seep while you sit and wait for your next breath.

Silence is another form of actively supporting and perpetuating these crimes. Miranda Yaver, a political scientist at the University of California, Los Angeles, and a veteran demonstrator aptly said during one of her demonstrations that "White silence = Violence". So someone needs to speak up loudly so that their voices don't go unheard like numerous times before. The list of the dead and the forgotten has been going far too. Their lives cannot be reduced to a trivial hashtag and conveniently forgotten until the next news cycle. The unjustified killings of the African American communities have to be stopped. Period.

The ripple effect of all the injustices towards the African American right from the day the Mayflower reached the shore, blood laced Civil Rights movement, racial profiling in traffic stops, to unnecessary use of violence in arrests, to disparity during the pandemic all of this has lead us to this moment. This inhumane moment in history where even breathing is considered a privilege for them. This is where humanity stands now. Nationally, the COVID-19 mortality rate for black Americans is two-point-four times higher than the rate for whites. Let that sink in.

Now the discrimination like the termite infested infection has slowly made its way to the highest level of the government and gnawing the very core of life, liberty, and happiness. Racial discrimination is so prevalent and keeps on widening when the leadership instead of acknowledging the angst and fear in the community is trying to widen it further. Instead of channelizing the fear and anxiety deeply seeded in the African American community, they are being brandished as a terrorist organization.

What do you say about the mendacious president who instead of calming and acknowledging burning angst in his country fellowman, turns off the light in the White House and hole up like a mouse in the bunker? This is what this land of the free and the home of the brave has been reduced to.

If you cannot step out of your homes and take part in a peaceful march or protest then you can raise money for bailing out the protestors who have been locked up.

Whether you are born with white privilege or any kind of privilege. Don't wait for the moment when you need to look for the hashtag to drive the attention of people towards you to make your life matter.

ACT NOW. SPEAK NOW.SUPPORT. DONATE

IWUAGWU IKECHUKWU

Lustre

Beyond the cracked sidewalk, and the telephone pole with layers of flyers in a rainbow of colors, and the patch of dry brown grass there stood a ten-foot high concrete block wall, caked with dozens of coats of paint. There was a small shrine at the foot of it with burnt out candles and dead flowers and a few soggy teddy bears. One word of graffiti filled the wall, red letters on a gold background: Rejoice!

The residents of Oakwood heights perhaps, saw the graffiti as a mirage, as it was more or less, next to unrealistic but then they had to hope for the best to come someday as it goes on to prove beyond reasonable doubt the saying which states that with life, there is hope. The burnt out candles and soggy teddy bears have been kept there deliberately as wreaths laid in respect of loved ones, lost to the aggressive environment either by drug and gang wars or by police brutality.

The assumption of a nationalist president, one might say could have ignited the various race incited violence, hate speech, and occasional sporadic shootings in places of worship, indeed one can't help but surmise that there was more to skin colour as it wasn't just a colour to some people.

It was barely a week into summer, the sun was on its path to retire in its abode below the horizon when Taylor stepped out from his house located in Oakwood Heights within the outskirts of Detroit to get some groceries from the store for his mum, Wonda, a nurse in her early forties who worked at the local pharmacy few blocks away from her ho use.

Taylor was sixteen years of age and in twelfth grade, living with his mom in their family house there in the suburbs after losing his father Jack barely six months ago during a crossfire between the Chicago police department (CPD) and some drug dealers after they were busted.

Jack and his family had returned from a summer vacation to Nairobi, Kenya in Africa, his hometown, and while on his way to work the following week, he was hit by a stray bullet fired by an eager cop at one of the drug cartel member, perhaps the most vicious amongst them known as "Sting" who had been marked by the cops as a ruthless and crafty fellow. He had been on their radar for so long a time and they couldn't afford to miss any opportunity to bring him to face the law, even if it meant shooting him.

The bullet had pierced Jack's chest region, rupturing the visceral artery, he had bled out profusely and eventually died on the spot as the police officers never paid attention to him but rather concentrated on the suspected drug cartel members who were engaged in a hot pursuit with the police, returning gunshots back to the police whenever they were at a convenient distance.

The blaring of an ambulance fifteen minutes later when it was clear that Jack had given up the ghost indeed reflected the high level of disdain and disrespect with which the black community was handled with. The ambulance crept up like a sluggish earthworm emerging from its moist hole, on arrival, they got down, took Jack's lifeless body and left, to the disappointment of onlookers

The pain of losing Jack to yet another stray bullet was quite difficult to drown in the ocean of discarded memories as it was felt by the whole neighbourhood where everyone looked out for one another irrespective of class. There was more to it than being neighbours, they were a community of people who felt each other's pain and celebrated each other's happiness.

If not for any other reason, Jack would be greatly missed by the fellow black families in Oakland heights as he always organized meetings amongst black families encouraging them to be strong and stand up to every wind of opposition, encouraging them to send their children to schools, and equally advised lads to avoid gang activities so that they can qualify and if possible represent them actively someday in congress and in effect, repress and suppress the wind of division sprouting amongst the populace. Jack was a symbol of peace in Oakland and as a result, his death was a great blow to every one of them.

It was indeed a fact that the community's population was dominated mainly by black families within the middle and lower class of the social strata. Repeatedly there have been rumors and subsequently some evidence on racial abuse by the police officers mainly of white descent and this of course, wasn't a good tiding.

During raids, police officers would always search thoroughly and in some cases try to implicate the houses occupied by blacks in the neighborhood and in turn, ignore houses occupied by the whites who were indeed few in number, it was always a moment black families dreaded, and therefore watched vigilantly to prevent themselves from being unjustly indicted.

Few weeks ago, a black lady was shot at point blank range, and another black man said to have been beaten to stupor by the police for what witnesses termed his refusal to allow his rights to be trampled upon, news of this sort always developed wings and always found itself causing panic amongst the young and feeble minded blacks in the state, as one couldn't help but ask if truly democracy is being practiced.

News of extra judicial killings always sent a chilly twitch down the spine of the average black individual on the streets and in the neighborhood as nothing was eventually done by the justice department to punish offenders, people could die innocently for crimes they didn't commit, the authorities in their usual manner would promise to get to the root of the matter, only to abandon it later.

There was indeed an urgent need for their voices to be heard,

"I mean aren't we humans like them!? This is unacceptable! We need real representation in congress"

Dwayne Hopkins, the newspaper vendor blurted out while reliving what real democracy should be like, he always reacted loudly to newspaper customers who gathered to go through the newspapers, he never cared if they responded or not, he was always ready to unburden his mind, he had been a newspaper vendor for over forty years and he never for once cared less to speak out against the ill treatment of the authorities even though it was obvious his opinions were not being heard.

Perhaps the dailies published in the past few years may have succeeded in painting the Oakwood heights as a danger zone with crimes such as gang wars, drug dealing, extortion amongst others, painting with negativity, the reputation of the once most loved neighborhood in the 90s.

Wonda would always relieve with Taylor how she met his father at the bar when their neighborhood was nothing but all shades of good and excellent, they would stroll the streets at night with hands interlocked as they both built their future with bricks of imagination until one evening when a drug war erupted as a result of a dealer who was said to have escaped with a huge quantity of cocaine and stashes of cash belonging to his boss to form his own drug cartel thereby starting a war which escalated and made Oakland heights never to remain the same.

This has over time, blown a bad wind upon residents of Oakland heights as job opportunities cum great investments are repelled by the negative image attached to the neighborhood which one could sum up as having transformed it to a semi slum. People were always advised to be careful when in the neighborhood as any unpleasant occurrence could take place impromptu, certain walkways were avoided at night, and in most cases, some streets.

Stories have been told of individuals who got shot or beaten up by police officers conducting investigations on the basis of mistaken identity, such was the case of six year old Shawn whose parents were killed right in front of him while they were taking a walk home.

The police officer who shot them had been earlier attacked by a black couple, perhaps, what the entire residents of Oakland heights would term a Bonnie and Clyde of the black community, which everyone usually laughed off as a joke, but subconsciously hoped that the acclaimed duo doesn't land them into costly problems someday.

The Chicago police department had declared the couple dangerously armed and to be shot at sight if it got to worse, indeed one might blame mother nature for making Shawn's parent share quite a striking resemblance with the most wanted couple that out of hatred and perhaps the quest to revenge the bullet wound sustained in his last encounter with them, Deputy inspector Logan on sighting them, gave a cynical grin, stepped down from his car, trailed them closely before catching up with them.

He approached stealthily from behind with a team of four junior officers, and without warning fired four shots point blank range at the innocent couple who dropped abruptly onto the floor as their trickling blood formed a creeping pool while they gasped for air before giving up in minutes.

Shawn never cried nor shivered but rather stood over the bodies of his parents now drenched in their pool of blood, staring at them as an angry mob began to materialize within minutes, one of the junior officers had called in an ambulance as ordered by

Deputy inspector Logan after which they got into the car and drove off, while waiting for the ambulance, a volunteer from the crowd tried using a piece of cloth to apply pressure to the couple even though it was obvious that his attempts were futile.

No doubt, like other black families in Detroit, Shawn's parents had prepared his tender and feeble mind for such moments as this. Surely, one could never know what tomorrow brings forth, indeed one could say that his parents did a wonderful job on a six year old from the way he conducted himself after this ugly incident must have unfolded in his very before, as the crowd increased, Shawn requested for a bullhorn from a fellow in the crowd who was a passerby probably on his way to make some announcements with it, and it was given to him.

The kid got up onto a milk crate and raised his hand. A murmur went through the crowd and then it fell silent, except for a few people shouting words of encouragement at him. The kid acknowledged them with a nod and a shy smile. In the full light of day, he looked less angry and more beautiful. He waited until people stopped shouting. A siren could be heard, maybe five or ten blocks away. The kid raised the bullhorn, pressed the button, and began to speak.

"Hello people"

He began

"My parents are dead, they have just been killed right here before you all, but my Dad had always told me that in the face of anything I should insist on doing the right thing and always show love, as well as being strong, brave, standing up to tough situations when such arises"

The crowd was shocked and marveled at such level of intelligence portrayed by a toddler and to be honest, most people amongst them agreed that they never had the level of confidence and boldness he had, they equally pitied the lad who would grow up in the absence of his parents who set him on the path of boldness.

Shawn led a protest to the Detroit Police Department. It might have paid off as Deputy Inspector Logan was demoted and suspended for six months, this wasn't a befitting punishment but in a place where subjugation and racism was the order of the day, it was perhaps to an extent a satisfactory measure and of course they dared not expect more, as it would end up a mirage or better still, an apparition.

One cool evening, when the sun had taken a dive into the horizon in retirement from the day's work, Taylor was walking down the quite lonesome street, putting on a hoodie with his hands tucked into the pockets on both sides, there was an occasional explosion of wind every now and then which seemed to kiss his cheeks as he walked rather briskly, dry leaves on the boulevard rose and fell with an occasional unique rhythm played by the wind's artistic gusto.

He finally got to the junction where he would make a final right turn to the grocery store, he heard an alarm blare behind him

That must be the cops

He thought

They must have been trailing me, but what the hell have I done?

He kept on walking confidently because like his late father once told him,

"One should never get scared for being innocent but rather for being guilty but in the face of all, you should stand your ground"

Immediately, the police patrol car stopped, a police officer stepped out of the car, standing authoritatively as he ordered.

"Freeze!"

The order came like a shock to Taylor as its syllables rolled out rather impatiently from the officer's lips

"Do not move, just turn around real slow!"

Taylor found himself in a pool of oxymoron, swimming between fear and boldness as he reminisced the words his father told him the morning of the day he was killed. Jack had always had a weird feeling that it was only a matter of time before the wave of racial violence got to his family or himself as one couldn't be sure of the form through which it will come. That morning, he had held sixteen year old Taylor's hand, looked into his eyes and charged him to be bold and strong at all times, as life barely had a place for the weak and feeble minded

"When challenges come, don't be afraid to stand your ground."

He had finally said before leaving the house. These words rang like a bell in his head as he turned around with his hands in his pockets facing the cops

" I was just going to get some groceries for my mom, I have done nothing wrong!"

He said putting up a bold face

"Let me see your hands in the air!"

The second officer thundered, and in a flash Taylor zoomed off and ran back towards his house as both officers followed suit in the hot pursuit. The first officer called for backup while the other concentrated on the hot chase. As Taylor was approaching the lane leading to his house, a deafening gunshot was heard, he dropped with a thud. He rose and ran rather slowly holding unto his right leg as blood trickled down, creating a trail

"I haven't done nothing!"

He protested repeatedly as he got to their door post and fell to the floor with a heavy thud, writhing in pain.

"Mom I've been shot by the cops!"

He screamed in pain in a bid to draw his mother's attention and in no distant time, a team of about thirty policemen arrived at the scene wielding gun's all drawn out pointed at him as they enclosed him.

Wonda opened the door, she was on her way to the pharmacy for her night shift, upon stepping out, she was shocked to her marrows, catching the terrifying glimpse of her son on the floor with a bullet wound and gun's pointing at him from all directions

"Do y'all wanna kill him!? What do y'all want from us!? I lost his Dad six months ago! He's all I got! Taylor is all I got!"

She exclaimed, shaking visibly. An officer drew closer, ordering him to stay still

"Keep your hands where I can see them, behind your back!"

Taylor grinned in pain as tears rolled down his cheeks, Wonda beheld him and for a moment wished she had the powers to change this ugly situation into a nightmare one could wake up from. Immediately, an idea struck her. She didn't care right now, all she wanted was for her son to be okay, she wanted peace. Wonda briskly went back inside her house and as the officer made a move to grab Taylor.

Suddenly, she emerged from the entrance with a bright red rose flower facing all the police officers who had their guns pointing at her son. Shocked and surprised they all exchanged glances with each other as she stood there pointing the flower at the Gun nozzle of the closest police officer to her standing between boldness, heartbreak and tears rolling down her cheeks, she kept bringing out more roses from the vase at the verandah adding it to the ones she had, a rose for each police officer until it totaled twenty.

She began soberly

"Love conquers everything despite tribe, religion, social class or race"

She went on in tears

"I know you all got sons, nephews, brothers and step sons his age, I swear his late father and I brought him up on the right path, he isn't into some kind of bad association because I try to provide his basic needs, can y'all do something good for God, his late dad and I by calling an ambulance please."

It was as though a hot knife was cutting through a sleeping butter bar as each of the police officers began to question their conscience. She stared into their faces

"You are a mother I guess, how would you feel if your son went in for what he knows nothing about?"

She said, pointing a rose flower stalk at the only female officer in the team

"We are one, no matter the race or social class."

She continued, boldly staring at her with a mixture of pity and fury. It was clear that Wonda's mode of protest was peaceful yet too hot for the average rational individual to ignore and within a minute they all lowered their guns and had an ambulance called in to evacuate Taylor to the nearest hospital to prevent him from losing much blood.

The Chief superintendent, Paul, a man of about fifty years of age went closer to Wonda and introduced himself and went further to apologize, he was emotional

"I'm so so..sor..sorry ma'am…"

He stuttered

"My deputy and I thought he was a gang member, I mean he ran when we stopped him, he made himself look like a suspect."

He continued with an air of regret

"We are currently carrying out an investigation on a major gang related murder, I mean, I have a son his age too."

He continued, almost in tears, Wonda saw his remorseful nature and hugged him

"You all just got to know that being irresponsible isn't race specific, I brought him up in a good way"

She said in between tears. For a moment the other officers felt awful and quite sad for almost taking the joy of this poor black woman away but again felt happy for not doing it, one could tell they were somewhat in a mood of regret mingled with happiness. It was as if the ground should retract its jaws and swallow them all, they were guilt stricken, a sharp arrow pierced and resuscitated their buried consciences from the dump of discarded memories, who knows, they might have been touched by her approach, charisma, or better still, her boldness. They were all enveloped in awe.

An officer from the team stepped forward, introduced himself as Lex from Brownsville Texas, he collected the flowers from Wonda and asked her to lead them to her late husband's grave, upon getting there he knelt down tearing up as he made some heart melting statements

"Hey Jack, I never knew you nor met you while you were alive but

I have met the most amazing black family ever and you got a brave boy out here, your wonderful wife had taught me today that love conquers all and I promise to personally look out for your little boy as long as I live."

He said, pensive, laying the thirty flowers altogether on Jack's tombstone, got up and hugged Wonda. One after the other, the remaining police officers hugged her as well occasionally parting with words of encouragements with gentle pats on her back, after which they slowly got into their various cars and drove off while the Chief superintendent waited with two other officers to drive Wonda to the hospital where she could go and check up on her son.

Wonda emerged from her house entrance, she found herself in a subtle mood, oblivious of how she should feel, tears rolled down her cheeks, a pensive mood enveloped her heart like a blanket as she wished her husband was alive to see the breakthrough made so far by the same community he once encouraged to be bold, now, here she was, two white police officers would drive her to the hospital to go and see her son, was she dreaming? Her mind raced through various assumptions as she got into the car. She was happy that the ugly fangs of division and subjugation are at the verge of being dismantled at least for now, more had to be done

It must not rear up its ugly head again.

She thought, as her mind raced between the thousands of upcoming generations whose minds and growth shouldn't experience this level of degradation and division, and her son Taylor who was probably enduring perhaps the highest level of pain for someone his age.

One could tell that the heavens stood still on that day because not just did the web of curiosity materialize a crowd in a few minutes. Of course, news such as this spread like wildfire within minutes, individuals of the neighborhood oozed out in their numbers in admiration of Wonda's bravery seeing her now not just as a mere individual, but as a role model, someone who had finally stood up to look death straight into its eyes on their behalf.

On arrival at the hospital, Wonda was shown the emergency room where her son was kept, she stared from the transparent partition. Taylor had been given a dose of anesthesia to relax him while the bullet was extracted. A doctor emerges soon from behind and introduces himself as Philip Woods.

"Your son is lucky and strong as well."

Dr Philip began with a professional aura

"The bullet almost shattered his right knee cap, this would have led to an amputation but like I said earlier, he was lucky, the bullet has been extracted and he will remain under our care for a month after which it would be safe for him to be discharged."

He continued confidently. Wonda was reassured for the time being, Taylor was all she had and she couldn't afford to lose him, it might kill her

"Can I see him now?"

She asked with a pinch of restored hope

"Yes, sure!"

Said the doctor as she walked in joyously, sat beside her son and held his hand firmly. Suddenly there was a very loud beep from the heart impulse monitor for some seconds which stopped abruptly and drew a straight line on the screen, a trickle of blood ran down his mouth and right ear, drenching his garment. Wonda's scream jolted even the dullest of hospital worker back to reality, the doctor rushed in followed by one of the nurses on duty only to declare Taylor dead after some quick examinations

"Ma'am you have to take it easy, he must have hit his head on the concrete which led to when he dropped to the floor after being shot, which led to internal bleeding and trust me, he lost a lot of blood. A bullet wound emergency was only reported by our new nurse whose shift ended moments ago. He must have failed to thoroughly examine him thinking that he passed out as a result of the bullet wound, we are sorry for your loss."

He said remorsefully, patted her back, and then walked away gently while the nurses present consoled her. It was as though a boulder, the size of the Eiffel tower was lowered unto her shoulders, tears rolled down her cheeks, she was dumbfounded

" Perhaps, I was destined to be alone."

She said amidst sobs, perhaps it was her fate. Predestination had once more tossed its dice.

JON C. MANNONE

Nothing's Changed

It's still the same old song: incivility shackles the spirit of any man. We are still slaves to socio-economics, to the perpetuity of greed, to gilded lies. It wasn't just the incivility of the Civil War—a cliché that no one will challenge.

Whom do we blame for our sins of racism still crouching at the door as a rabid dog? Our masters? I too am indecent, my heart—a gnarled trunk sunk in deep mud. Yet my tears run clear, they flow for the disenfranchised, for the homeless and for my brother, white or black.

Where are the champions, the abolitionists of social injustice? I think they're mired deeper in quicksands of false morality; they're even worse than the slave owners. They seem to be more interested in political gain.

I feel the immortality of their stone-cold hearts, the immorality of riots incited in the name of righteousness, riots that *they* had conjured by their indifference, so many, many times. Even now—Los Angeles, Fergusson, New York, Baltimore, Charleston, Atlanta, Minneapolis—we still burn with incivility in all the world, not just in our cities or between our states, the same behavior that tore this nation into tatters, then gray and blue but now mostly the frayed color of our hearts that are still being mended, still stained with the blood of so many young men.

It is no different now than it was then: while the Southern ladies raised their glasses with dainty cotton-gloved hands, then sipped their mint, sweet teas while gossiping who they saw at the ball (who was waltzing with whom), the slaves, with their finger-pricked hands, loaded cotton into the gin that danced to the scrim and sway of rubber belts in the feculent heat.

END

SARA WHITESTONE

Being wrong, being right, and being a white woman of privilege

In a small Virginia town I mistakenly make an illegal U-turn. A police officer immediately pulls me over. I immediately start crying. These are not crocodile tears; instead they flow from the mortification that I did something wrong and will have to (rightfully) face the consequences.

And yet, there are no consequences. I am a white woman crying in front of a white policeman who doesn't even ask for my driver's license. Instead, he waves me off and says, "Just be more careful out there, ya hear?"

Charles is a black man who is walking along a sidewalk in Miami. Without warning, two white policemen come up behind him and slam him against a wall. "Are you gonna be a problem?" one of the officers asks.

Even after they take their hands off Charles, they don't excuse their physical violence; rather they try to defend it by saying Charles fits the description of a wanted black man.

Both of these stories are true. And what also is true is this: As a white woman, I have never once worried about police bullying. But as a black man, this wasn't the first time Charles has been roughed up. And if things don't change, it won't be his last.

For years now I have heard variants of the pithy argument that if you don't want to get in trouble, you shouldn't do anything wrong. I did something wrong with my illegal U-turn, but I wasn't issued a ticket. Instead, because of my privileged, white-woman status, I drove away free.

In contrast, Charles did nothing wrong. He was simply a black man walking down a street who was manhandled just because of his skin color.

I teach writing at John Jay College of Criminal Justice, part of the public City University of New York system. Because of the makeup of our students, I am often the only white person in the classroom. And I am aware of my power—not just as a professor who evaluates student performance, but also as a privileged white woman who has not had to face the racial bias and abuse that, because of their diversity, my students experience almost daily.

And because of my privilege, I check in with myself daily—questioning if I have perpetrated even the slightest abuse of power in my classroom. While I acknowledge that I will never fully understand the inequalities my students must combat, I try to stand with them in solidarity and to reach toward them with empathy.

When my students are feeling powerless, I reassure them that—soon— the people-of-color minority will become the majority. I also explain that some in the current white majority are fearful of losing their social dominance, and that fear often manifests itself in violence.

Being verbally supportive of my students in a classroom where I have power is easy. But the question I keep asking myself is this: If I had been there—watching a white policeman use his knee to strangle George Floyd—would my love for that dying human have been compelling enough for me to take action? Would I have risked my own safety by using my white-woman privilege to try to stop the murder?

Honestly, I don't know. Yet, I hope this questioning of myself will strengthen my resolve to not just say the next right thing, but, regardless of the consequences, actually *do* the next right thing—whatever that may be.

KASAK JAIN

The Colours My Skin Holds

I am being raised in a world where the colours we are coloured with instead of making us unique and special, they make us less or more than the other, building a patriarchy of its own. I am expected to accept one and reject the existence of the other. I am expected to prefer one and consider it superior while stripping away the dignity of the other. No one says it but ignores it altogether. But are we not the children of this Earth, our World? Are we not born in the same way or empty our lungs in the same way?

We all come in colours- from the evening sun to the awakening night; From the alluvial soil to the fine snow. But without the sun, the moon cannot shine in the night; Without the soil, can no land and mountains be formed.
Yet we continue to judge the people, wholly based on what covers their body.
We say we are in a much better place when it comes to racism but is that not denial in its purest form?

We give birth to it everyday, by mocking a person for his colour, by being bystanders to it everyday. And soon a child grows up thinking, thinking it is normal- that the colour one's skin holds matters.

the society weeps today with the land, skies, mountains, rivers.

But we can change it. We can stop it when it happens. A simple no, a strong resistance to it, can bring a difference that will change us and the forthcoming generations forever.

JEFF KNORR

Monopoly

In Minnesota a man with an outstanding warrant was pulled over and offered officers a Get Out of Jail Free card.

The Telegraph—July 24, 2017

Un fucking believable flashes across his face when he reads the card—you'd think the guy told him he was Pablo Escobar. But, you see, this is a card we should all carry—hell, the cop carries one—you think that his driver's license isn't next to his badge so when one of his cop buddies pulls him over drunk on the highway—well, there it is you see. He doesn't get a K-9 released on him, the run and grab, bit hard at the shoulder, held, a gun to the back of his head—no, no, no dash cam rolling, no chest cam, no breathalyzer pulled out on that stop, *head home, head home, take it is easy, baby*—I like justice, we all do, we all want the guy doing something real wrong to get his, but come on, when it stops working that way, and we know it has, well then, we want the night to open up for everybody, we want the streetlights to shine evenly on that pavement of the American Dream—the long road home, past the trees and stars. Get us all out of jail free, change the bail system so my American brothers and sisters, sons and daughters, felons and the fabulous can go home to their families—not just the rich, not just the exalted, not just, not just…but free, make us all free, free us from all our skin our flesh and rotten meat, our bones. Free. Free.

ROGER COLLINS

Humanoid Traffic Stop
A Ten-Minute Play by Roger Collins
Playwright's notes:

This play requires one scene and five adult characters: two police offi-
cers in a police squad car, two passengers in a vehicle that's been pulled
over, and one Robocop (a robot police officer). The vehicles can be
represented by chairs with the occupants seated side by side. Custom-
ary casting would have the driver male and his passenger, female. The
Robocop wears a policeman's cap (as do the officers in the squad car)
and futuristic sunglasses (eyeshield).

Cast

ROBOCOPi
COP 1
COP 2
DRIVER (African American male)
PASSENGER (African American female)

At Rise

ROBOCOP lumbers from the squad car, toward the vehicle pulled-
over. There is enough distance between ROBOCOP and the passenger
car that several lines of dialog can be exchanged before ROBOCOP
reaches the passenger car. ROBOCOP walks and talks "somewhat"
robotically – but not melodramatically so. The DRIVER and PAS-
SENGER do not initially recognize ROBOCOP as a robot. The PAS-
SENGER is preoccupied with her cellphone, presumably accessing

GPS directions.

At Rise
PASSENGER (female)

(Waving her cellphone)
You don't even know where we are, do you?

DRIVER (male)

Don't start that again!

PASSENGER

(Looking back at ROBOCOP)
And now this!

COP 1

(Observing ROBOCOP)
He's moving way too slow!

COP 2

It! How many times do I have to tell you? It! It's moving way too slow!

COP 1

Okay, okay! It's moving way too slow! I wanted to test the omni-wheeled model, but nooo –

COP 2

The omni-wheel's faster – but too fast. Scary fast! I bet at least one driver shoots it when it gets
field tested.

DRIVER

(Looking back, shouting
toward ROBOCOP)
Any day now!

COP 1

See! He's supposed to – I mean, it's supposed to have a calming influence. Assure the driver. But this thing's moving too slow to be calming!

PASSENGER

(To DRIVER)
Can you believe how slow he's walking? He's trying to intimidate us!

DRIVER

(To ROBOCOP)
Got no one else to harass this morning?!

ROBOCOP

That's okay – I understand. You're exercising your first amendment right. Freedom of speech. I know the law!

DRIVER

Know this!
(Gives ROBOCOP the finger;
PASSENGER restrains him.)

COP 1

This ain't going well! Call it back!

COP 2

Let's wait!
(Points to a "screen" in the squad car)
It's scanning perfectly. It recorded the license number, our location, the
number of occupants –

ROBOCOP

(Finally reaches the car
pulled over; to DRIVER)
I don't think you even slowed down at that stop sign back there.

DRIVER

Of course, I did!

ROBOCOP

Okay. Okay. You slowed down, but you didn't stop.

PASSENGER

He did, too! I'm in the car – I should know!

ROBOCOP

(Points to cell phone in
PASSENGER'S hand.)
You might have been preoccupied. Distracted, perhaps. (Beat). This situation, this incident, this occurrence, shall we say – it offers a teachable moment. I'm reminded of a parable I'd like to share.

COP 1

A parable? Who programmed this thing?

DRIVER

And you're supposed to know the law? You wanna recite a parable? Ever hear of separation of church and state?

ROBOCOP

This is a secular parable. It's allowed! (Beat) There once was a driver.

PASSENGER

(To ROBOCOP)
Good God! Just give him a ticket!

DRIVER

Whoa – wait. If we listen to this parable, can I just get a warning?
ROBOCOP

Well, I do have discretion. My artificial intelligence does not mean fake intelligence.

DRIVER

Wait...what?
(Then, to
PASSENGER)
This thing's a robot!

ROBOCOP

Wait...what? That isn't obvious? You couldn't tell? It defeats the purpose if traffic violators can't tell!

DRIVER

(Leaning away from ROBOCOP)
Purpose? The purpose? What purpose?

ROBOCOP

To reclaim public trust!

PASSENGER

With robot cops?

ROBOCOP

Absolutely! For one, you'll notice I'm unarmed. That's a huge plus for
many citizens. And even though I'm unarmed, I'm pretty much inde-
structible, keeping human police out of harm's way. I can protect and
serve even while under attack!

PASSENGER

You're still a robot!

ROBOCOP

(Waves ticket
book at DRIVER.)
With the authority to issue tickets. Without bigotry, I might add. I'm
robotically unbiased!

DRIVER

Okay, okay...I'm willing to listen to your parable if you just give me a
warning.

ROBOCOP

Well, no promises. This is a full-service traffic stop.

PASSENGER

Full service?
(To DRIVER;
waving cellphone)
Should I record this?

DRIVER

(Shaking his head.)
No, no...let's not...you know. Let's just listen.

ROBOCOP

Well there once was a driver...

PASSENGER

Jeez!

ROBOCOP

...and this driver approached a stop sign, slowed down, looked both
ways, and drove right
through it.

COP 1

You know where this is going?

COP 2

No clue.

ROBOCOP

They didn't see the police officer a half block away, but the officer saw them. The officer turns on the siren and flashes the red-and-blues, pulls them over, and asks the driver for license and registration.

DRIVER

We getting close to the parable part?

ROBOCOP

(Leans inside the car)

COP 1

(To COP 2)
What's it doing?

DRIVER

(Leaning away from ROBOCOP)
What...are...you...doing?

ROBOCOP

Okay – just as an aside, before I go on with my parable.

PASSENGER

Oh my Lord, why me?

ROBOCOP

Most citizens don't realize that traffic stops are a fantastic way for us cops to find what we're really looking for. Something spectacular! You know, illegal weapons. Burglary tools. Drugs.

COP 2

(To COP 1)
It can sniff for dope. Explosives. Nervous sweat, even. Electronically, of course.

COP 1

(To Cop 2)
Jeez...you think it could replace us?

ROBOCOP

(Removes head from "car."
Resumes former posture.)
Well...where was I?

COP 2

(To COP 1)
They must be clean.

ROBOCOP

Oh yeah – the officer gets the driver's license and registration. Asks if the driver was in a hurry. Emergency maybe? We cops aspire to be understanding. Ideally, of course. But this driver claims no emergency and appears unrepentant. Arrogant even. Sees no difference between slowing down and looking both ways and coming to a full stop. And perhaps there is no major difference safety-wise. But words have mean-ing, no? And slowing down is not the same as coming to a full stop. So the officer pulls the driver from the car, takes out his baton, and begins to beat the driver over the head.
(DRIVER & PASSENGER
recoil from ROBOCOP)

COP 1

Who wrote its software?

ROBOCOP

And while the officer's beating the driver he asks – a rhetorical ques-tion, mind you – would you like me to stop .... Or...would you like me to slow down? Get it? Stop or slow down?

DRIVER

Are you freakin' crazy?

PASSENGER

Dammit! I coulda recorded that! A Robocop parable!

ROBOCOP

And it is just that, ma'am – a parable. That couldn't actually happen.
(Sotto voce, striking fist into palm.)
Although... if the baton were made of soft rubber...
(Beat. Back to normal voice)

But you do get the point, right?

DRIVER

Yeah, yeah – I get it. Stop sign. Full stop. Understood. (Pause) Can we
go now? You know, with that warning you promised?

ROBOCOP

No, no – no promise, remember? Full service. So, first, your license
and registration.
(DRIVER hands over papers)
(ROBOCOP reviews papers)

ROBOCOP (continued)

(Nodding approval)
Okay, okay. (Pause) You know your rear tag light is broken.

DRIVER

My what?

ROBOCOP

Your rear license plate light. Broken.

DRIVER

It's daylight for God's sake! I don't have my lights on!

ROBOCOP

Nevertheless, your rear tag light is broken. When you do turn on your lights, your rear tag light won't work.

(ROBOCOP lumbers to the back of the car,
looks down, and taps its sunglasses/eyeshield.)

ROBOCOP (Continued)

Refractometry. That's how I know. Please...don't ask me to explain the science. Take my word for it: your rear tag light is broken!

COP 1

(To COP 2)
No, really! You think it could replace us?
(The low hum of a gathering crowd murmurs

from behind the audience. The hum continues
at moderate volume until the end of the play.)

DRIVER

Okay. Okay. Full stop at stop signs. Replace my rear tag light. Now
can we go?

ROBOCOP

After a gentle reminder. Just as a point of emphasis. You could have had
an emergency. One that required urgency. Emergencies can happen to
anyone. How you handle them – that's the key. You'd hate to turn an
emergency into a tragedy. By plowing into someone. Another car. Or a
pedestrian. Not to mention throwing a monkey wrench into your hope
to make haste in the first place! Can you imagine? Hitting somebody?
Killing somebody? The guilt. The remorse. The lifelong regret.

COP 2

(To COP 1)
Yeah – this is getting weird.
(Points to the audience)
And....we're beginning to attract attention.

COP 1

(To COP 2)
Time to pull the plug!

COP 2

(To COP 1)
But I'd like to avoid the shaming!

COP 1

(To COP 2)
Shaming? This thing's got feelings?

COP 2

(To COP 1)
Yeah – this model, anyway. That's where it gets its empathy. Or so I've
been told. (Beat.) I know – I'll blame it on our car's computer. Yeah,
that's it – a computer malfunction…
(To ROBOCOP)
Officer Weller!ii
(Points to a "screen" in squad car.)
We got a glitch here in our computer system. We'll take it from here!
(COP 1 leaves the vehicle.
COP 2 fingers the car's console,
deactivates ROBOCOP, and
joins COP 1 outside the car.)

ROBOCOP

(To COP 1 and COP 2)
Let me do my job, damnit!
(PASSENGER leaves her

vehicle and begins to record
on her cellphone, panning
between cops and the audience.)

COP 1

(To COP 2)
Turn it off! Turn it off, damnit!

COP 2

I did! I did turn it off!
(Only the low hum of the crowd is heard
in the background. COP 1 & COP 2 initiate
body cam recording and scan between
ROBOCOP and the audience.)

ROBOCOP

(Walking toward,
facing audience)
I want everybody to back up. That's right. Back up, please. Nothing to
see here. Just back up and stay calm. Easy, now, easy. That's right. No
need to panic. Easy. No one has to get hurt.

END OF PLAY

Endnote:

i The character name, Robocop, pays homage to the character in the film (Davison, J., Ver-
hoeven, P., Weller, P., Allen, N., & Orion Home Video. (1987). Robocop. New York, N.Y:
Orion Home Video), but is clearly NOT the same character thereby avoiding complications
regarding any trademark that might exist. Later reference is made to Peter Weller as homage to
the actor who played the original Robocop in the film.

BEN FINE

GIVE ME A TICKET OR LET ME GO

I realize that it is a difficult time to be for a police officer in this age of Black Lives Matter, Stopping unknown people, which is necessary for a cop, is a tension raising experience. However interactions with the police, even for law abiding citizens, are never a pleasant experience. Consequently most people develop a negative image of police, whether black or white. White people, like myself, realize how truly frightening police interactions are for black people. This is a story of how a policeman drew his gun on me, a white college professor.

Most police officers are dedicated civil servants. However, anyone who has observed cops in action , has seen that many have a chip on their shoulders and a distinctive us versus them attitude. It seems that to the average cop, everyone, other than another officer, is a potential perp and the officers respond accordingly. When a person is stopped for a traffic infraction, there is no need for the officer to be nasty, you were caught that's all. Yet the normal result is being treated as if you were a criminal.

Before I get to my story I must say that this police attitude is particularly bad if you happen to be black. This is the whole point of Black Lives Matter. A friend of mine, who is a black school principal and whose wife is an assistant school superintendent, live in a high end Connecticut town. After the Michael Brown shooting we were discussing police attitudes to all black people. Despite his very large income, he told me that he couldn't buy his son, a very good high school student, either too nice a car or too cheap a car. If he bought him a BMW or some car like that, which he could well afford, there would be a 100% chance that his son would be stopped and hassled by the local police, On the other hand if he bought him a cheap used Toyota there would also be a 100% chance of being stopped, because of the large poorer neighboring city. As a result he had to buy him a middle of the road car, a used Camry, to avoid the police hassles. Each black father talks of the police talk he has to have with his son, unfortunately to keep him alive.

My own story happened in 1974. During the previous decade, the sixties, there were the frequent hippies versus pigs confrontations, that cemented bad blood between police officers and anyone with long hair. By 1974, my semi hippie years were long behind me. I was already a professor of mathematics at a good university with a wife and a daughter, but I still had long bushy hair.

I had played golf with a friend of mine and on the way home we stopped in at a McDonalds in downtown Brooklyn. I was driving an older semi- beat up blue Buick with Connecticut plates. I sat in the car while my friend went inside to pick up the food.

Suddenly a police car pulled up behind me and a police officer came to my window.

    "License and registration please." The officer told me.
I was just sitting there so I asked him,"What did I do? " I received no answer just another
    "Give me your license and registration"
I knew not to fight with a police officer, so I handed them over to the cop. He looked at my

Connecticut license and said "I know that you have an expired New York license and I'm going to get you" It was ridiculous. But I said nothing as he walked back to his patrol car. Luckily for me he had a partner.

He kept me sitting in my car for about twenty minutes. My friend came back from the McDonalds and asked me what was going on. I told him "I don't know. Out of the blue he asked me for my license and registration. He told me that I had an expired New York license and he was going to get me."

After another ten minutes, I got out of my car and began walking towards the patrol car. The officer shouted out of his window "Get back in your car."

Again, I didn't fight with him and walked back to my car and sat back down.
He then kept me there another thirty minutes just sitting. Unfortunately I have a bad temper and by this point I was quite pissed. I got out of my car and walked to the patrol car.
    He again yelled "I told you to get back in your car."
This time I ignored him and I walked to his window and said
    "I did nothing. Either give me a ticket or let me go."
He got out of the patrol car and stood eye o eye with me
"I told you to get back into your car." He bellowed.
I was royally pissed so I guess this could be considered my fault. He again told me "get back in your car" now completely nasty. I repeated to him.
    "Either give me a ticket or let me go.

He suddenly pushed me and force of reaction I stupidly pushed him back. My hot temper had taken over. I was on the US army boxing team and was unfortunately the type of person who took no shit from anyone. I had just pushed a cop so I imagine the nightstick should have come out and he would hit me with it. Instead, like Wyatt Earp, he pulled his gun from his holster and pointed it at me..

I stepped back in fear, pretty much shitting in my pants.

Suddenly his partner walked over and surprisingly grabbed him by the arm and turned the gun away from pointing at me. If I was black he probably would have shot me already. The partner said something to him and then the partner walked over to me. The partner handed me my license and registration and briefly said told me "Get out of here" The officer who pulled the gun on me must have been some sort of psycho.

My friend and I quickly drove off with my heart still pounding from seeing a gun pointing at me.

ACKNOWLEDGMENTS

"Guilt by Omission: A Call to Arms" A version of this poem first appeared in As the World Burns: Writers and Artists Reflect on a World Gone Mad from Indie Blu(e) Publishing

"Visiting Albany" originally appeared in The Dribble Drabble Review #1.

"Old Order Supremacy" previously published via Headline Poetry and Press.
Photo: Capitol Hill Autonomous Zone, June 13, 2020

"The Readiness Is All" was first published in *Calyx* in 1995.

"Being wrong, being right, and being a white woman of privilege" first appeared online in Rock and Sling, June 2020.

"Blue Code of Silence" Publication credit: Barzakh, Spring 2017 issue, ed. Victorio Reyes

Collins, R. (2020) *"Humanoid Traffic Stop,"* Astral Waters Review, Spring, Issue 3, 40-52.

"One Night" appeared in the summer issue of The New Ohio Review, 6/17/2020

"Welcome to the Neighborhood" first appeared in Solstice Literary Magazine

"A Short Poem on the Shooting by Police of Charquisa Johnson" Margie/The American Journal of Poetry

"Three-Hour Reprieve" Forpoetry.com

"It Was My Mother Who Taught Me to Fear" originally appeared in Poetry Salzburg Review 37

"My Mother, the Police, and Me" The first publication of this poem was in HEArt (Human Equity Through Art) and was reprinted in my collection, How I Learned To Be White.

"An Act of Self Defense" (Subterranean Blue Poetry)

"A Nation in Chokehold" (As the World Burns, Indie Blue Press, 2020)

"Peace - a metaphor for denial" (Poetry Diversity 2020)

"Bless us lord for the sin-free life we are living" ("Lift Every Voice" by Kissing Dynamite Press)

"Don't Wait Till You Become a Hashtag" (Lumiere Review, 2020)

"White House Rodeo" The first stanza of this poem was published in La Bloga, on Feb. 27, 2018, as *"Choke Hold Sonnet."*

"Still I Breathe" was published in the Anthology- Aporajito Das in India.

CONTRIBUTORS

Millicent Borges Accardi, a Portuguese-American writer, is the author of two poetry books, most recently Only More So (Salmon). Her awards include fellowships from the National Endowment for the Arts (NEA), Fulbright, CantoMundo, Creative Capacity, the California Arts Council, The Corporation of Yaddo, Fundação Luso-Americana, and Barbara Deming Foundation, "Money for Women."

Iris De Anda a Guanaca Tapatia poet, speaker & musician has been featured with KPFK & KPFA Pacifica Radio, organized with Academy of American Poets, performed at Los Angeles Latino Book Festival, Feria del Libro Tijuana, Casa de las Americas in Havana, Cuba and is named one of Today's Revolutionary Women of Color. Author of Codeswitch: Fires from Mi Corazon.

Imogen Arate is an award-winning Asian-American poet and writer and the Executive Producer and Host of Poets and Muses, an award-winning weekly poetry podcast. She has written in four languages and published in two. Her work was most recently featured in The New Verse News, dyst Journal and KJZZ's (Arizona's NPR affiliate) 'Word' podcast.

Taofeek Ayeyemi fondly called Aswagaawy is a Nigerian lawyer and writer whose works have appeared in Lucent Dreaming, Ethel-zine, the QuillS, The Pangolin Review, Modern Haiku, Hedgerow, Acorn, Akitsu Quarterly, Seashores, contemporary haibun online and elsewhere. He won Honorable Mention Prize in 2020 Stephen A. DiBiase Poetry Prize, 2019 Morioka International Haiku Contest and 2nd Prize, 2016 Christopher Okigbo Poetry Prize among others. His chapbook "Tongueless Secret" (Ethel Press) and full-length book "aubade at night or serenade in the morning" (FlowerSong Press) are forthcoming in 2021.

Catharine Batsios (she/her or they/them} is from Flint, MI & currently lives in Detroit where she is a Poet & Teaching Artist serving Detroit youth & the Detroit literary community. It took her 8 years & 1 drop-out to graduate from a State school. She studies with the Daedalus Poets, et al at the Kitchen Table of Diane Wakoski. Find her poetry at Glass Poetry, Flypaper, Linden Ave Lit, Kissing Dynamite's Punk Anthology, & more. Her poems are the intimacies of the cities that have built her, things you consider trash but she doesn't, & empathy as told through strange non-verbal gestures.

Sonia Beauchamp (she/her) is a healing artist and the daughter of a Chinese immigrant. Her writing often explores multiracial identity and growing up in the Deep South. Read her recent work in *Anomaly, pioneertown,* and *Maudlin House.* Find out more at www.soniakb.com.

Nandini Bhattacharya was born and raised in India and has called the United States her second continent for the last thirty years. Her novel *Love's Garden* was published in October 2020 and has garnered positive reviews. Her work has been published or will be in Sky Island Journal, the Saturday Evening Post Best Short Stories from the Great American Fiction Contest Anthology 2021, The Bombay Review, Meat for Tea: the Valley Review, Storyscape Journal, Raising Mothers, The Bangalore Review, PANK, OyeDrum, and more. She has attended the Bread Loaf Writers' Workshop and been accepted for residencies at the Vermont Studio Center, VONA, Centrum Writer's Residency, and the Ragdale Artist's Residency (forthcoming), among others. She was first runner-up for the *Los Angeles Review* Flash Fiction contest (2017-2018), long-listed for the Disquiet International Literary Prize

(2019 and 2020), a finalist for the Reynolds-Price International Women's Literary Award (2019), and received Honorable Mention for the Saturday Evening Post Great American Stories Contest, 2021.

She's currently working on a second novel about love, minorities, racism, and Hindutva politics in India and xenophobic mentalities and other mysteries in Donald Trump's America, titled Homeland Blues. She lives outside Houston with various other living things.

Andrea Blancas Beltran is a writer and artist from El Paso, Texas. Her work has been selected for publication in *The Offing, Borderlands: Texas Poetry Review, Poetry Northwest, Scalawag,* and others. You can find her @drebelle.

Chris Billings is a member/co-chair of the Sun Poet's Society in San Antonio, TX, as well as co-host for their weekly open mics. He has had poems included in several anthologies and has self-published four chapbooks. He lives in Schertz, TX.

jo reyes-boitel is a poet, essayist, and playwright. jo is also a queer, mixed-Latina parent working in community. jo's work includes <u>Michael + Josephine</u>, a novel in verse (FlowerSong Press, 2019), and <u>mouth</u> (Neon Hemlock, Summer 2021), as well as the operetta *she wears bells*. Recent publications include The Ice Colony, OyeDrum, Scalawag Journal, and Chachalaca Review. jo currently serves as advisory editor for FlowerSong Press and guest editor with Red Salmon Press.

Michael Brautigan lived most of his life in and around the Bay Area. He lived for over a decade in Berkeley, where he participated in protest activism and community awareness groups, and graduated from UC Berkeley with a degree in English Literature. He has been published in Milvia St. Journal, Unlikely Stories, Control Literary Magazine, Red Fez,

Return to Mago E*Magazine, Dm du Jour, and Carcinogenic Poetry and was a member of online groups such as New Surrealist Institute, Inter Dada, Global Writers, Poets, and Artists, and the accidental poet.

Lisa Braxton is the recipient of a 2020 Outstanding Literary Award from the National Association of Black Journalists for her debut novel, The Talking Drum. Her stories and essays have appeared in anthologies and literary magazines including Vermont Literary Review, Black Lives Have Always Mattered, Chicken Soup for the Soul and The Book of Hope. She is a fellow of Kimbilio, a fellowship for fiction writers of the African diaspora, and an Emmy-nominated former television journalist.

Ernie Brill writes fiction and poetry about everyday people. His for "I Looked Over Jordan and Other Stories" explores race and class among hospital workers. The actress Ruby Dee purchased, adapted, and performed one of the stories" Crazy Hattie Enters Ice Age" for a PBS TV series.
FBrill won a New York State Council For The Arts Fiction Grant
Mr. Brill received his BA and MA in English from San Francisco
Brill has published widely fiction,poetry and essays and in the US and Canada(River Styx, Other Voices, Z, U. of Minnesota, Prentice Hall Ontario Canada.
Favorite writers include Virginia Woolf, Richard Wright, Mahmoud Darwish, Hyseoon Kim, Gwendolyn Brooks, Sterling A. Brown, and Pablo Neruda.

Jeff Cannon: A U.S. New England poet, author of Intimate Witness: The Carol Poems (Goose River Press, 2009), Eros Faces of Love and Finding the Father at Table (X-Libris, 2010). I was an ever-present attendee (until recently due to health issues) at the "Dirty Gerund Poetry Show" at Ralph's Diner. It is the place that became my poetry home to celebrate music and the gifts of many young poets and musicians. Other publishing credits include Goose River Anthology (2009 & 2014) and Boundless 2014 & 2020 (El Zarape Press), and Another Year Living Under the Dragon Stars (FlowerSong Press, 2021).

Vanessa Caraveo is a bestselling and award-winning bilingual author and published poet who has been avidly involved in writing throughout the years. She is involved with various organizations that assist children and adults with disabilities and enjoys working with non-profit groups to promote literacy. Her work brings focus to many social issues that exist in today's world and has been published in *The Chachalaca Review, The Raven Review, Literature Today Journal* and for various anthologies in which she aspires to make a positive difference by uplifting the lives of others through her literary work.

Robin Carstensen's poetry manuscript, *In the Temple of Shining Mercy* received the annual first-place award by Iron Horse Literary Press in 2016. Her poems are recently published or forthcoming in *Voices de La Luna, Acting Up: Queer in the New Century*, by *Jacar Press*, and many more. She directs the creative writing program at TAMU-CC where she is faculty advisor for *Windward Review: Literary Journal of the South Texas Coastal Bend*, and co-founding, senior editor for *Switchgrass Review: Literary Journal of Health and Transformation*.

Emenike Christian Chijioke is an illustrious Nigerian, an essayist and young African visionary leader making a difference in the society. He's a sage whose sagacity is directed towards making the system that drives the progress of humanity better.

He is the founder/leader of The Sagacious Tribe; a group of young talented minds with the mission of inspiring, encouraging, and motivating all and sundry with their talent.

Enjoys thinking, inking and inspiring. A sage, motivator, poet, ferocious leader, life coach, inspirational writer and speaker.

Roger Collins is an African American psychologist and professor emeritus at the University of Cincinnati where he received the university's Cohen Award for Excellence in Teaching. His short fiction has been published in a variety of literary journals, and his stage plays produced in Cincinnati and Dayton, Ohio, Fort Thomas, Kentucky, and in Brooklyn, NY.

Dawn Corrigan's poetry and prose have appeared widely in print and online. Her masthead credits include Western Humanities Review, Girls with Insurance, and Otis Nebula, where she currently serves as assistant editor. She works in the affordable housing industry and lives in Myrtle Grove, FL. Find her online at www.dawncorrigan.com.

Dr. Ron Craig is a retired psychology professor, most recently assisting students, and many students of color, achieve their Associate degree at Cincinnati State College. He resides in Batavia, Ohio, USA. Since 2016 his haiku and senryu have been published in numerous journals, anthologies and blogs. As an Ohio Certified Volunteer Naturalist he practices stewardship at the Cincinnati Nature Center. Married, with one adult daughter, he is honored to be included in this important anthology of poems collected by Flowersong Press.

Linda M. Crate's works have been published in numerous magazines and anthologies both online and in print. She is the author of six poetry chapbooks, the latest of which is: *More Than Bone Music* (Clare Songbirds Publishing House, March 2019). She's also the author of the novel *Phoenix Tears* (Czykmate Books, June 2018). She has published three full-length poetry collections *Vampire Daughter* (Dark

Gatekeeper Gaming, February 2020), *The Sweetest Blood* (Cyberwit, February 2020), and *Mythology of My Bones* (Cyberwit, August 2020).

El Davíd is a NuYorican poet from the Bronx, NY and author of poetry collections "Growing Up Rican," and "Hip Hop Made." He is the NY Taino Awards 2016 "Areito Poet of the Year.;"
His works have been published in the anthologies, "Me No Hablo With Acento" edited by Emanuel Xavier, "The Bandana Republic" edited by Luis Reyes Rivera & Def Poetry Jam co-founder Bruce George, and the August 2019 "Acentos Review: Performance of Breath" edition edited by Lupe Mendez & Peggy Robles-Alvarado. He has had featured readings at the National Black Theatre, Nuyorican Poet's Cafe, Bowery Poetry Club, Bronx Museum for the Arts, Great Weather for Media, Teatro Latea, and El Museo Del Barrio. El is the founder of Urban Beat Poet Society, a non-profit organization whose mission is to create platforms for writers and artists through workshops, performances, music productions and publications.

Within the Lockdown, **Mike Ekunno** has had works published in *Mysterion, The Blue Nib, Oddball Magazine* and *Written Tales* with pending anthology publications in *Essential Anthology* of Underground Writers Association of Portland, Main, and *Omens Anthology* of Antimony and Elder Lace Press. He is a freelance book editor, ghost biographer and author of Cowboy Lamido, a children's book approved as school text across Nigeria. Mike venerates the late Mohammed Ali and is a massive fan of the defunct ABBA which doesn't make him New School by any means.

Dr. Ben Fine is a mathematician and professor at Fairfield University in Connecticut in the United States. He is a graduate of the MFA program at Fairfield University and is the author of sixteen books (twelve in mathematics, one on chess, one a political thriller, one a swahbuckler about pirates and a romanic comedy) as well over 130 research articles, fifteen short stories and a novella about Pirates. His story *August 18,1969* published in the Green Silk Journal was nominated for a Pushcart prize. His story *From the Dambovitsa to Coney Island* was an honorable mention winner in the Glimmer Train Literary Contest. His story "The Schuyler Diamonds" won First Place in the Writer's Digest Popular Fiction Awards in the Mystery/Crime Category. His story "My Mother, God and the Big Blue Ford", published in Green Silk Journal won Honorable Mention in the 45th New Millennium Writing Awards. He has completed a memoir told in interwoven stories called *Tales from Brighton Beach: A Boy Grows in Brooklyn.* The stories detail his growing up in Brighton Beach, a seaside neighborhood on the southern tip of Brooklyn, during the 1950's and 1960's. Brighton Beach was unique and set apart from the rest of New York City both in character and in time. His latest novel *The Salsa KIng if Sxarsdale* was released in 2020. His author website is https://benfineauthor.com

Jonathan Fletcher, an alumnus of the North East School of the Arts and Our Lady of the Lake University, has been published in *Lone Stars, TEJAS COVIDO, The Thing Itself,* and *Voices de la Luna.* He currently resides in San Antonio, Texas.

Thomas Fucaloro The winner of a performance grant from the Staten Island Council of the Arts and the NYC Department of Cultural Affairs, Thomas Fucaloro has been on six national slam teams. He holds an MFA in creative writing from the New School and is a co-founding editor of Great Weather for Media and NYSAI press. He is an adjunct professor at Wagner College and BMCC where he teaches world lit and advanced creative writing. His latest chapbook, "There is Always Tomorrow" was released in 2017 by Mad Gleam Press. Thomas' forthcoming chapbook, "The Only Gardening I Do is When I Give Up" by Poets Wear Prada, is due winter 2020.

Martina Gallegos was born and raised in Mexico and came to the United States at 14. She got a Master's degree from Grand Canyon University after a near fatal hemorrhagic stroke . Her works have appeared in the Altadena Anthology: Poetry Review 2015, 2017, 2018, Hometown Pasadena, Spirit Fire Review, Poetry Super Highway, Vocal media, Silver Birch Press, Central Coast Poetry Shows, Basta! and more recently, in the award-winning anthology, When the Virus Came Calling: COVID-19 Strikes America. Published by Golden Foothills Press, editor, Thelma T. Reyna.

Crystal Garcia is a Corpus Christi native who graduated in 2012 although strives to continue her education in being a student of life. She is a lover of books and all things literature—especially poetry. Crystal is also the co-creator of a local podcast called Revolve One. Through this platform, Crystal along with her brother and podcasting partner, Rudy, seek to connect with their local community and listeners from all around the world. Whether through the podcast or her writing, Crystal exercises her ability to pen heartfelt poetry and also confronts with veracity the current events of our time. In everything she does, this writer and content creator expresses empathy as well as an unfaltering love for creative endeavors.

She's **America Garcia**. She loves fashion, film, and writing. She's also a former university student majoring in both theatre and marketing. She plans to become both a fashion designer, film director, and an author. She wants to influence others to not be afraid of pursuing what they want to do. She wants to create change and make an impact in this world.

Lorraine Garnett was born in Jamaica. She is a member of PEN America: Worker Writers School. Lorraine's first interview was with Journalist, Maddie Crum of The Buffler, for a piece titled, Meditations in an Emergency. Lorraine is a nanny and lives in Brooklyn with her college scholars, Laurence and Paris.

Christian Garduno's work can be read in over 55 literary magazines. He is the recipient of the 2019 national Willie Morris Award for Southern Poetry. Christian Garduno is a Finalist in the 2020-2021 Tennessee Williams & New Orleans Writing Contest. He lives and writes along the South Texas coast with his wonderful wife Nahemie and young son Dylan.

Michael Gerleman is an English teacher in South Texas.

Tammy Melody Gomez is a performing artist, writer, and grassroots activist whose literary work—essays, poetry, microfiction—has been published in numerous collections, including *Bikequity: Money, Class, and Bicycling* (Microcosm Publishing, 2017) and *Entre Guadalupe y Malinche: Tejanas in Literature and Art* (UT Press, 2016). "SHE: Bike/ Spoke/Love" (2007), her NALAC-funded play, depicts the Latinx bicycling culture, and her one-woman show, "Saliendo Abierta,"premiered at the Mexican American Cultural Center (Austin) in 2009. Tammy is profiled in Las Tejanas: 300 Years of History (UT Press, 2003), and is a member of the Macondo Writers Workshop.

"Black Hole," written in the early 1990s, is the first of numerous pieces Tammy has written and performed that confront the carceral state and the prison-industrial complex, as well as race- and class-driven acts of violence by the boys in blue. She has performed this particular poem—to music composed by her band La Palabra, and as an a capella hip hop piece—in cities across the country, including a courtroom at the juvenile detention center in Austin.

Jim LaVilla-Havelin is the author of five books of poetry, the most recent of which, WEST, poems of a place (Wings Press, 2017), examines his move from city life to the country.
His work has appeared in many Texas Poetry Calendars, anthologies of work about Selena, Bob Dylan, popular music, and Moby Dick. Educator, editor, and community arts activist,
LaVilla-Havelin is the Poetry Editor for the San Antonio Express-News/ Houston Chronicle and the San Antonio Coordinator for National Poetry Month activities and calendar.
He was the City of San Antonio's 2019 Distinction in the Arts: Literary Arts awardee, and the 2019-2020 Gemini Ink Writing Instructor of the Year.

Ryan Havely earned his BA in English from Ohio University and his MFA in Creative Writing from Minnesota State. He taught English at WVU-Parkersburg for nearly a decade, and now works in sales and marketing. His work can be found in such magazines as Main Street Rag, Ampersand, Pebble Lake Review, and Midwestern Gothic.

Mark Andrew Heathcote is adult learning difficulties support worker, his poetry has been published in many journals, magazines and anthologies, he resides in the UK, from Manchester, he is the author of "In Perpetuity" and "Back on Earth" two books of poems published by a CTU publishing group ~ Creative Talents Unleashed.

hector son of hector dreams of short stories and speaks in verse. He is originally from Long Beach, CA but now lives in Oakland. He writes in English and throws in Spanish sin traducciones. He grew up working class and his parents are from Mexico—he pulls on those strings for inspiration. He works in a hospital and writes poetry in secret, hoping his words are louder than his person.

G.G. (Giana Gallardo) Hesterberg was born and raised in Brownsville, Texas, and graduated from the Fine Arts Program at Lopez High School in 2000. She studied at Central College in Pella, Iowa, and received a Bachelor's degree in Elementary Education in 2004. She published her first book, *Stories by the Seashore,* in March of 2019. Her second book, *Music, Music, You Can Too!,* a nonfiction children's book, was released in July 2020. Hesterberg lives in South Texas with her husband, three children and a dog.

Iwuagwu Ikechukwu is an African poet, essayist, screenwriter, budding dramatist and graduate of English and Literary studies. His poems won the Poetry Nook weekly contest and got an honourable mention respectively, published in the fifth paperback edition of the Poetry Nook anthology, available on amazon. His short story "Five Shades of Victory" was awarded an honourable mention in the IHRAF Creators of Justice award in New York - 2020 edition, His works have been published in The Shallow Tales Review, Black Boy Review, Talk Afro Magazine & Ka'edi Africa (Nigeria), Jalada Anthology: Nostalgia issue (Kenya), About Place Journal, Flora Fiction and Fumble Magazine (USA), Dissonance Magazine (UK) and Orange Blush Zine (Malaysia). A foodie and lover of the Igbo culture, amongst his hobbies are researching, writing, studying, reading of African literature as well as engaging in creative and thought provoking arguments.

Emmanuel Ikuoye is a graduate of University of Ibadan, Nigeria. He is an essayist, short story writer and poet whose major preoccupation is balanced on the tripod of equality of mankind irrespective of race, social justice and crusade against corruption.

James Croal Jackson (he/him/his) is a Filipino-American poet. He has a chapbook, *The Frayed Edge of Memory* (Writing Knights Press, 2017), and recent poems in *Sampsonia Way, Los Angeles Review of Los Angeles,* and *Pacifica.* He edits *The Mantle Poetry* (themantlepoetry.com) and works in film production in Pittsburgh, PA. (jamescroaljackson.com)

Spoken word poet/author, **Brandon L. Jackson,** is a black queer writer who advocates self-love, love for others and healing through the power of expression. A graduate of Sam Houston State University, he is the author of four poetry book collections; "The Parts Medicine Can't Reach" Volumes 1 & 2, "Somewhere Between Logic & Emotion" and "From A Sky's View".

Continuously evolving, Brandon has traveled the states performing, been a featured guest on the Internet talk radio show "The Journey" hosted by Neville Deangelou, featured in the anthology Blues Arrival: Stories of the Queer Black South & Migration, performed in rallies for LGBT equality such as "RevLove", has had his words featured in the art exhibit called "Blues Talk: It Ain't No Chit Chat Cliché" by visual artist/community activist Vicki Meek and has had reoccurring performances for The T.R.U.T.H. Project, led by Kevin Anderson, that provides artistic outlets for HIV awareness within the community.

Kasak Jain is a young writer and has been writing for a long time now. Jain says, "For me, art is a better understanding of life and existence, perhaps, the difference between existing and living. I also have a page on instagram(@kasakwrites) and that is the platform I usually use to enhance my skills.

Milton Jordan, lives in Georgetown, Texas, with his wife the musician

Anne Elton Jordan. He has published essays, poems, reviews and stories in literary and general circulation journals. His latest poetry collection is *What the Rivers Gather,* Stephen F. Austin University Press, 2020.

Tricia Knoll is a Vermont poet who spent many years digging into the history of her family, childhood and training to unpack the role of white privilege in her life. Her collection How I Learned To Be White earned the 2018 Indie Book Award for Motivational Poetry. More poetry on her website: triciaknoll.com

Jeff Knorr is the author of four books of poetry, *The Color of a New Country* (Mammoth Books, 2017), The *Third Body* (Cherry Grove Collections), *Keeper* (Mammoth Books), and *Standing Up to the Day* (Pecan Grove Press). Jeff was the Poet Laureate for the city and county of Sacramento from 2012-2016. He lives in Sacramento, California and is Professor of literature and creative writing at Sacramento City College.

John C. Krieg is a retired landscape architect and land planner who formerly practiced in Arizona, California, and Nevada. He is also retired as an International Society of Arboriculture (ISA) certified arborist and currently holds seven active categories of California state contracting licenses, including the highest category of Class A General Engineering. He has written a college textbook entitled Desert Landscape Architecture (1999, CRC Press). John has had pieces published in A Gathering of the Tribes, Alternating Current, Blue Mountain Review, Clark Street Review, Conceit, Homestead Review, Line Rider Press, Lucky Jefferson, Oddball Magazine, Palm Springs Life, Pegasus, Pen and Pendulum, Saint Ann's Review, The Courtship of Winds, The Mindful Word, The Writing Disorder, and Wilderness House Literary Review. In conjunction with filmmaker/photographer Charles

Sappington, Mr. Krieg has completed a two-part documentary film entitled Landscape Architecture: The Next Generation (2010). In some underground circles John is considered a master grower of marijuana and holds as a lifelong goal the desire to see marijuana federally legalized. Nothing else will do. To that end he has two books coming out this year being published by Ribbonwood Press entitled: *Marijuana Tales* and *More Marijuana Tales*.

Laurie Kuntz is an award-winning poet and film producer. She taught creative writing and poetry in Japan, Thailand and the Philippines. Many of her poetic themes are a result of her working with Southeast Asian refugees for over a decade after the Vietnam War years. She has published one poetry collection (*Somewhere in the Telling*, Mellen Press) and two chapbooks (*Simple Gestures,* Texas Review Press and *Women at the Onsen,* Blue Light Press), as well as an ESL reader (The New Arrival, Books 1 & 2, Prentice Hall Publishers). Her poetry has been nominated for a Pushcart Prize, and her chapbook, Simple Gestures, won the Texas Review Poetry Chapbook Contest. She was editor in chief of *Blue Muse Magazine* and a guest editor of *Hunger Mountain Magazine.* She has produced documentaries on the repeal of the Don't Ask, Don't Tell Law, and currently is producing a documentary on the peace process and reintegration of guerrilla soldiers in Colombia. She is the executive producer of an Emmy winning short narrative film, *Posthumous.* Recently retired, she lives in an endless summer state of mind. https://lauriekuntz.myportfolio.com/home-1

Originally from Saskatchewan, **Allan Lake** has lived in Vancouver, Cape Breton Island, Ibiza, Tasmania & Melbourne. Poetry Collection: Sand in the Sole (Xlibris, 2014). Lake won Lost Tower Publications (UK) Comp 2017 & Melbourne Spoken Word Poetry Fest/The Dan 2018. Poetry Chapbook (Ginninderra Press, 2020): My Photos of

Sicily.

Peggy Landsman is the author of a poetry chapbook, To-wit To-woo (Foothills Publishing). Her work has been published in numerous literary journals and anthologies, including The Muse Strikes Back (Story Line Press), Breathe: 101 Contemporary Odes (C&R Press), Nasty Women Poets (Lost Horse Press), SWWIM Every Day, Mezzo Cammin, and The Ekphrastic Review. She lives in South Florida where she swims in the warm Atlantic Ocean every chance she gets. https://peggylandsman.wordpress.com/

D.L. Lang served as the poet laureate of Vallejo, California (2017-2019). Her work has appeared in Colossus:Home, A Poet's Siddur, and Light & Shadow. She has performed hundreds of times since 2015 at protest rallies, county fairs, and literary events. She is the author of 13 books of poetry and the editor of Verses, Voices, and Visions of Vallejo. You can find her online at **poetryebook.com**

Mark Lipman, is the founder of VAGABOND (www.vagabondbooks.net) and the Culver City Small Press Book Festival; recipient of the 2015 Joe Hill Labor Poetry Award; winner of the 2016 International Latino Book Awards for The Border Crossed Us (an anthology to end apartheid); editor and publisher of RISE (an anthology of Power and Unity) and EXTREME (an anthology for social and environmental justice); a writer, poet, multi-media artist and activist, is the author of nine books, most recently, The Role of the Revolutionary Poet in Society and a Strategic Vision for the 21st Century; Imposing Democracy; Poetry for the Masses; and Global Economic Amnesty. His work has also appeared in notable international anthologies such as, 21 Poetas por la Paz, (21 Poets for Peace), (Universidad Juárez Autónoma de Tabasco) and Coiled Serpent, (Tia Chucha Press). Co-founder of the

Berkeley Stop the War Coalition (USA), Agir Contre la Guerre (France) and Occupy Los Angeles, he has been an outspoken critic of war and occupation since 2001. Mark uses poetry to connect communities to the greater social issues that affect all of our lives, while building consciousness through the spoken word. Currently, he is the Vice-Chair of Culver City's Committee on Homelessness and is a board member of POWER (People Organized for Westside Renewal); member of the IWW (Industrial Workers of the World), Ground Game LA, Veterans for Peace, Occupy Venice, the Revolutionary Poets Brigade, 100 Thousand Poets for Change and the World Poetry Movement.

Jack e Lorts has published widely, if infrequently, the past 50+ years in magazines & more recently online, i.e., Arizona Quarterly, Kansas Quarterly, English Journal, Haggard and Halloo versedaily, etc. His most recent book is "The Love Songs of Ephram Pratt" from Uttered Chaos Press. His "Ephram Pratt" poems appear widely online.

John C. Mannone has poems in *North Dakota Quarterly*, *Azahares*, *Acentos Review*, *Sin Fronteras*, 2016 *Texas Poetry Calendar*, *Le Menteur*, *Poetry South*, *Baltimore Review*, *Wordpeace*, and others. His poetry won the Impressions of Appalachia Creative Arts Contest (2020). He was awarded a Jean Ritchie Fellowship (2017) in Appalachian literature and served as celebrity judge for the National Federation of State Poetry Societies (2018). He edits poetry for *Abyss & Apex* and other journals. A retired physics professor, he lives near Knoxville, Tennessee.

Lucinda Marshall is the Founder and Host of the DiVerse Gaithersburg (MD) Poetry Reading, and the Founder and Facilitator of the Gaithersburg (MD) Poetry Workshop. Her poetry has won awards from Waterline Writers, *Third Wednesday*, and *Montgomery Magazine*, and has been published in numerous journals, including *Global*

Poemics, *Broadkill Review*, *Foliate Oak*, *The Rising Phoenix Review*, and *Poetica*, as well as in the anthologies "Poems in the Aftermath" (Indolent Books), "You Can Hear The Ocean" (Brighten Press), "Is It Hot In Here Or Is It Just Me?" (Beautiful Cadaver Project), and "We Will Not Be Silenced" (Indie Blu(e) Publishing). You can learn more about Lucinda on her website, LucindaMarshall.com.

Nick Maynard is a queer urban creative living and working in the North of England. His work has appeared in a number of publications and exhibitions, both virtual and physical. Check out his on-line curated feed @ShadowmanPropa1

Bob McNeil, writer, editor, and spoken word artist, is the author of *Verses of Realness*. Hal Sirowitz, a Queens Poet Laureate, called the book "A fantastic trip through the mind of a poet who doesn't flinch at the truth." Among Bob's recent accomplishments, he found working on *Lyrics of Mature Hearts* to be a humbling experience because of the anthology's talented contributors.

Mr. Mills holds an MFA from Warren Wilson College. He's published three collections, *The Dream Detective, The Sudden Country* and *After Mistic* (Massachusetts slavery poems). His poems have been published in Ploughshares, Colorado Review, Crab Orchard Review, Newtown Literary, Jubilat, Callaloo, Brooklyn Rail and Fence. He has also received fellowships from the New York Foundation for the Arts, Breadloaf and the Lannan Foundation. He has recorded his poetry on RCA records and ESPN and lived in Langston Hughes' landmark Harlem home for three years.

M. Anthony Miranda came of age in the border communities of Southern Texas. He was born in 1974 and was raised in what is commonly referred to as the mid-Valley where upon receiving a Bachelor of Arts in the fall of 1999 took his first teaching job at Weslaco East High School. Much of his experiences growing up in a border town comprise the true depth of his writing, choosing often to join the vast majority of South Texas authors in illustrating the effects of institutional structures upon the traditionally marginalized and under-represented border communities where Miranda and his people still reside.

Kathleen Murphey is an associate professor of English at Community College of Philadelphia. She is a poet and fiction writer as well as a visual artist. Her visual art has been featured through Headline Poetry and Press, Virtual Imaginations: COVID-19, and other platforms. For more information go to, www.kathleenmurphey.com.

Tom Murphy's books: *Pearl* (FlowerSong Press 2020), *American History* (Slough Press, 2017), co-edited *Stone Renga*(Tail Feather, 2017). Murphy is *Langdon Review*'s 2021 Writer-In-Residence. Forthcoming work in *Switchgrass Review, Langdon Review, Writing Texas, Locus Review, Corpus Christi Writers, Concho River Review, Good Cop/Bad Cop Anthology* and *Wine.* Murphy has been named the 2021-2022 Corpus Christi Poet Laureate.

Brandon Nisbet is a Navy veteran and is a student at Florida international university. When he isn't writing he is spending time with his Daughter Kehlani and his dog Koi.

Gabriel González Núñez was born in Montevideo, Uruguay, and is currently a translation professor at UTRGV. He has published poetry, children's books, and short stories, mostly in Spanish. As a poet, he has authored a collection titled *Ese golpe de luz* (FlowerSong Press 2020) and a digital, bilingual chapbook titled *El ciclo / The Cycle* (2020), made possible through a grant from the Center for Latter-day Saint Arts. He has also published poems in journals (e.g., *The Chachalaca Review*) and anthologies (e.g., *Boundless*). His poem "Un dios en quien confiar" was included as part of a literary recital titled *Thorns & Thistles* (2019). As a children's author, he has published six books (and counting) in a collection titled *Me llamo…* (Penguin Random House Uruguay 2019, 2020). As a short story writer, he has authored several stories, which have been published in print and online magazines. He was awarded the 2012 Platero Award by the UN Spanish Book Club for his short story "El viaje que no se dio." Other short stories have been finalists or received honorable mentions in different contests.

Kendra Nuttall is a copywriter by day and poet by night. Her work has appeared in *Spectrum*, *Sad Girl Review*, *Capsule Stories*, *Chiron Review*, and *What Rough Beast*, among various other journals and anthologies. She is the author of poetry collection, *A Statistical Study of Randomness* (Finishing Line Press). She lives in Utah with her husband and poodle. Find her online at kendranuttall.com.

Chidiebube onye Okohia is a Pushcart-nominated Nigerian writer, poet and artist. He is the author of the chapbook, Of Dark Tides and Darkling Times. A graduate of English from the University of Lagos, some of his works have been published by Counterclock, Crow Name, Juke Joint, The Confessional, The Shallow Tales Review, The Daily Drunk, fresh.ink, Farafina, The Kalahari Review, and elsewhere. He tweets at @o_okohia.

Chinedu Vincent Okoro is a Nigerian writer, poet, playwright, social change activist and an educator. He holds a B.Ed in Educational Management and Political Science from Enugu State University of Science and Technology (ESUT), Nigeria.

TEDx Speaker and Pushcart Prize nominee **Daniel García Ordaz**, a.k.a. The Poet Mariachi, is the author of *Cenzontle/Mockingbird (YA Edition): Songs of Empowerment* and *You Know What I'm Sayin'?* He teaches at La Joya Early College H.S. García, a native of Mission, Texas, is a former newspaper journalist and a Navy veteran. He's available for author events and is on social media as @poetmariachi.

Connor Orrico is a student and field recordist interested in global health, mental health, and how we make meaning from the stories of person and place we share with each other.

Juan Manuel Pérez, a Mexican-American poet of indigenous descent and the current Poet Laureate for Corpus Christi, Texas (2019-2020), is the author of several books of poetry including two new books, SPACE IN PIECES (The House Of The Fighting Chupacabras Press, 2020) and SCREW THE WALL! AND OTHER BROWN PEOPLE POEMS (FlowerSong Press, 2020).

Alan Perry is the author of the poetry chapbook Clerk of the Dead, published by Main Street Rag Publishing in 2020. His poems have appeared in Tahoma Literary Review, Heron Tree, Sleet Magazine, Gyroscope Review, Zingara Poetry Review and elsewhere, and in several anthologies. He is a Senior Poetry Editor for Typehouse Literary Magazine, and was nominated for Best of the Net. Alan holds a BA in English from the University of Minnesota, and he and his wife divide their time between Minneapolis, Minnesota and Tucson, Arizona. More at: https://alanperrypoetry.com

DaRell Pittman is a performance poet who resides in San Antonio Texas. This husband, father and grandfather believes in the power of words to change the world. "They can teach and educate. Incite and inflame. Calm and soothe. Arouse and stimulate. Devastate and demolish. Inspire and elevate. Words are vehicles that move civilizations and direct humanity. Moreover, the written word is the closest thing we have to making ourselves immortal. And that, says DaRell Pittman, "is a powerful concept."

Bonnie Price
Poet name: Chinazo Dayo
70s baby, Lover of Motown, 80s and & 90s R & B
Self published novella Bitter Honey
Married mom of two, Fierce Grandmother of 3
Proud HBCU grad

Dave Rendle is a poet based in Cardigan, West Wales, a Welsh speaker currently without work, but committed to the ethos of solidarity and freedom. He is a member of local poets who, once a month, meet and perform under the name 'The Cellar Bards'. He is actively involved in his local Amnesty International Group, and is a keen blogger, under the name 'teifidancer'. His work has been published in Red Poets and in the online blog ' I am not a silent Poet'

Dimitri Reyes is a Puerto Rican multidisciplinary artist, YouTuber, organizer, and educator from Newark, New Jersey. He has organized large-scale poetry events such as #PoetsforPuertoRicoNewark and read at venues such as The Dodge Poetry Festival, Split This Rock, Busboys and Poets, and the American Poetry Museum. Dimitri's forthcoming book, Every First and Fifteenth is the winner of the Digging Press 2020 Chapbook Award. His work has been nominated for Best of the Net and you can find some of his writing in Vinyl, Kweli, Entropy, Duende, Cosmonauts, Obsidian, & Acentos. He is the Marketing &

Communications Director at CavanKerry Press and is an Artist-in-Residence with the New Jersey Performing Arts Center. Learn more about Dimitri by visiting his website at https://www.dimitrireyespoet.com/

Dr. Zack Ritter received his PhD from UCLA in Higher Education, researching racial stereotypes of Asian International Students, worked at American Jewish University as a Career Center Director, University of Redlands as a Assistant Director of Diversity, Harvey Mudd College as Dean of Diversity, and now at Cal State Dominguez Hills as Associate Dean of Students. He has co-authored two books, both about Whiteness and Challenging the Status Quo in Higher Ed. He has also written on Jewish and Black solidarity movements and is a Diversity Consultant, helping schools, businesses, and orgs imagine how to create Anti-Racist cultures and systems

Gerard Robledo is a Latino social justice poet from San Antonio. He holds an MFA in Creative Writing from the University of Texas at El Paso, and teaches creative writing at San Antonio College. His Spanish language poetry translations, poetry, and book reviews have appeared in *Voices de la Luna, the Texas Poetry Calendar, The Texas Observer, Pilgrimage, The Thing Itself, Outrage: A Protest Anthology for Injustice in a post 9/11 World,* and *Poetrybay,* among others. Robledo is also one of the first sixteen poets to be archived in the newly established San Antonio Poetry Archive at Palo Alto College and is a Macondo Writers' Workshop Fellow.

Rod Carlos Rodriguez (formerly Stryker), B.A. in Creative Writing, is an award-winning poet who has been writing for over 38 years. He has 3 books of poetry published and is founder/chair of the Sun Poet's Society, South Texas's longest running weekly open-mic poetry reading. He was nominated for the San Antonio Poet Laureate in April 2012,

April 2014, April 2016, and April 2018. He is also the poetry editor for the Ocotillo Review, a literary journal/periodical published by Kallisto Gaia Press.

David A. Romero is a Mexican-American spoken word artist from Diamond Bar, CA. Romero is the author of My Name Is Romero (FlowerSong Press 2020), a book reviewed by Gustavo Arellano (¡Ask a Mexican!), Curtis Marez (University Babylon), and founding member of Ozomatli, Ulises Bella. Romero has appeared at over seventy-five colleges and universities in over thirty different states in the USA. Romero was the second poet to be featured on All Def Digital. Romero has opened for Latin Grammy winning bands Ozomatli and La Santa Cecilia. Romero's work has been published alongside poets laureate Luis J. Rodriguez, Jack Hirschman, Alejandro Murguia, and Lawrence Ferlinghetti. Romero has won the Uptown Slam at the historic Green Mill in Chicago; the birthplace of slam poetry. Romero has appeared in-studio numerous times on multiple programs on KPFK 90.7 FM Los Angeles. Romero's poetry deals with family, identity, social justice issues, and Latinx culture.

Michael Rothenberg is co-founder of 100 Thousand Poets for Change and co-founder of Poets In Need, a non-profit 501(c)3, assisting poets in crisis. His most recent books of poetry include *Drawing The Shade* (Dos Madres Press, 2016), *Wake Up and Dream* (MadHat Press, 2017), *I Murdered Elvis* (Alien Buddha Press, 2020), and a bi-lingual edition of Indefinite Detention: A Dog Story (Varasek Ediciones, Madrid, Spain, 2017). An Arabic edition of *Indefinite Detention: A Dog Story*, trans. by El Habib Louai was published in Cairo, Egypt by Arwiqa Publishers in 2020 He lives in Tallahassee, Florida where he is currently Florida State University Libraries Poet in Residence.

Jonathan Rowe is a writer and copyeditor from Boston, Massachusetts. His writing has been published in Black Fox Literary Magazine, Sojourners, The Ekphrastic Review, Arkansas Review, and elsewhere. Jonathan's poetry has been exhibited in Boston City Hall and he has been selected to participate in Mass Poetry's U35 Reading Series. You can learn more about his work at jonathanrowewrites.com.

Yolanda Sealey-Ruiz is an award-winning associate professor at Teachers College, Columbia University. Her research focuses on racial literacy in teacher education, Black girl literacies, and Black and Latinx male high school students. A sought-after speaker on issues of race, culturally responsive pedagogy, and diversity, Sealey-Ruiz works with K-12 and higher education school communities to increase their racial literacy knowledge and move toward more equitable school experiences for their Black and Latinx students. Sealey-Ruiz appeared in Spike Lee's "2 Fists Up: We Gon' Be Alright", a documentary about the Black Lives Matter movement and the campus protests at Mizzou. Her first full-length volume of poetry, Love from the Vortex & Other Poems, was published in March, 2020 (Kalediscope Vibrationss LLC).

David Salner's first novel, *A Place to Hide,* will appear in 2021 from Apprentice House.
His latest poetry collection is *The Stillness of Certain Valleys* (Broadstone Books, 2019). His stories and poems have appeared in many journals including *Threepenny Review, Ploughshares, Beloit Poetry Journal, Carve,* and *The Moth (U.K.).* He worked as iron ore miner, steelworker, machinist; now as librarian.

Raúl Sánchez is the newest City of Redmond Poet Laureate 2020-2021. He teaches poetry in Spanish at Evergreen High School through the Seattle Arts and Lectures (WITS) program, also at Denny

International Middle School through the Jack Straw Educational Project and volunteers for PONGO Teen Writing at the Juvenile Detention Center. Currently he translated Ellen Ziegler's book for the Museum of Antique Mexican Toys.

Jeanie Sanders is a poet and collage artist. She lives in Lytle, Texas. Her poems have been published in The Texas Observer, San Antonio Express News, Texas Poetry Calendar, Voices de la Luna, Austin International Poetry Festival Anthology, La Voz de Esperanza, 100 Thousand Poets for Change, 'Women Speak' Anthology, Mutabilis Press Anthology: Enchantment of the Ordinary,and The Larger Geometry Anthology. Her book of poetry is called, 'The Book of the Dead' Poems and Photographs. She is the Poetry Editor for the 2021 Texas Poetry Calendar.

Gerard Sarnat MD's won San Francisco Poetry's 2020 Contest, the Poetry in Arts First Place Award/Dorfman Prizes; has been nominated for a handful of recent Pushcarts/Best of Net Awards; authored HOMELESS CHRONICLES (2010), Disputes, 17s, Melting The Ice King (2016). He's widely published including recently by academic-related journals Stanford, Oberlin, Wesleyan, Johns Hopkins, Harvard, Pomona, Brown, Penn, Dartmouth, Columbia, , 2020 International Human Rights Art Festival, Sichuan, Canberra, Universities of Chicago and Maine; as well as Ulster, Gargoyle, Main Street Rag, Northampton Poetry Review, New Haven Poetry Institute, Peauxdunque Review, American Journal Poetry, Vonnegut Museum and Library Literary Journal, Poetry Quarterly, New Delta Review, Buddhist Poetry Review, Brooklyn Review, Texas Review, LA Review, San Francisco Magazine, New York Times. Mount Analogue selected KADDISH for distribution nationwide Inauguration Day. Poetry was chosen for a 50th Harvard reunion Dylan symposium. Gerardsarnat.com

James Schwartz is a poet, writer, slam performer and author of 5 poetry collections including The Literary Party: Growing Up Gay and Amish in America.
He currently resides on Nisqually land (Olympia, WA.)
http://literaryparty.blogspot.com @queeraspoetry

Emily Shearer is an ex-pat poet and yoga/French/writing teacher. Her poems have been nominated for Pushcarts and "Best of"'s, and published in Silk Road Review (forthcoming), Kestrel, Please See Me, jellybucket, Fiolet & Wing, emry's journal online, psaltery & lyre, West Texas Literary Review, Clockhouse and Ruminate, among others. You can find her on the web at https://www.bohemilywrites.net.

Nancy Shiffrin is the author of 3 poetry collections: The Vast Unknowing, Infinity Publishing, BN.com, 2012; Game With Variations and Flight forthcoming from wordpoetrybooks.com. Her novel, Out of the Garden is available from lulu.com along with an essay Invoking Anais Nin.

Ndaba Sibanda's poems have been widely anthologised . Sibanda is the author of The Gushungo Way, Sleeping Rivers, Love O'clock, The Dead Must Be Sobbing, Football of Fools, Cutting-edge Cache: Unsympathetic Untruth, Of the Saliva and the Tongue, When Inspiration Sings In Silence and Poetry Pharmacy. His work is featured in The Anthology House, in The New Shoots Anthology, and in The Van Gogh Anthology, and A Worldwide Anthology of One Hundred Poetic Intersections. Some of Ndaba`s works are found or forthcoming in Page & Spine, Peeking Cat, Piker Press , SCARLET LEAF REVIEW6, Universidad Complutense de Madrid, the Pangolin Review, Kalahari Review and Botsotso.

Megha Sood lives in Jersey City, New Jersey, USA. She is an Assistant Poetry Editor for Literary Journal MookyChick(UK), Cross Tree Press (USA), and a Literary Partner in the *"Life in Quarantine"* Project by Stanford University, California, USA. Works widely published in journals including Better than Starbucks, Dime Show Review, Oddball Magazine, Poetry Society of New York, WNYC Studios, Kissing Dynamite, Dime show review, and many more. Works featured/upcoming in 50+ other print anthologies by the US, UK, Australian, and Canadian Press. Three-time State-level winner NAMI Dara Axelrod NJ Poetry Contest 2018/2019/2020, National Winner Spring Robinson Lit Prize 2020, Finalist in Pangolin Poetry Prize 2019, Adelaide Literary Award 2019, TWIBB Beyond Black Sakhi Awards 2020, etc. Currently co-editing the anthologies (*"The Medusa Project"*, Mookychick), and (*"The Kali Project"*, Cross Tree Press). She blogs at https://meghasworldsite. wordpress.com/ and tweets at @meghasood16.

Jason D. Söderblom is an Australian writer and lawyer. His analysis of rule of law, democracy, and the inequities affecting the poor, vulnerable and marginalised influences many of his publications including his non-fiction essays, short stories, and poetry.

Erika Elisa Garza Tamez is originally from the magic town Cd. Mier, Tamaulipas, México. She immigrated to the United States when she was fifteen years old. She holds a Bachelor's and Master's Degree of Arts in Spanish from UTPA with a thesis in creative writing. Garza is currently a Spanish Dual Instructor for La Joya ISD and South Texas College. Her poems have been published in Cuícatl, FEIPOL Anthology 2018, Boundless 2019, Boundless 2020, Dreaming: A Tribute to Selena Quintanilla-Pérez, RevistaTierra Firme, FAME RGV Magazine, Flora Fiction Literary Magazine, 6to Encuentro de Poetas de Cupatitzio, Mariposas sin primavera, among others. She has participated in literary meets from Argentina, Chile, Colombia, México, El Salvador, Spain, United States and Uruguay.

Chuck Taylor was raised in Texas, Minnesota, Illinois, and North Carolina, and won the 1988 Austin Book Award for What Do You Want, Blood? His latest are Being Beat (2018) , and I Tried To Be Free (2020), both published by Hercules Press.

Taylor worked in the Poets-in-the-Schools program in the 1970's, served as CETA Poet-in-Residence of Salt Lake City in the 1970's, operated Paperbacks Plus in the 1980's, runs Slough Press with Christopher Carmona from 1973-2020, and was Creative Writing Coordinator at Texas A&M. He also taught at UT Austin, UT El Paso, and UT Tyler, as well as in Japan.

Today he lives in the Texas hill country on the border between the South, the West, and MexAmerica. Taylor loves to swim in and canoe the local spring fed San Marcos River. He is also a photographer and a children's magician.

Karen Tardiff has been writing since she could hold a pen. She writes poetry, flash fiction, personal essays, short stories, and grant requests. She has been published in a variety of online and print outlets. She was born in Texas, lived a little bit of everywhere, and now resides on the Texas Gulf Coast. She is the founder of the Aransas County Poetry Society and Publisher/Editor-in-Chief of Gnashing Teeth Publishing. When she can't find poetry somewhere, she puts it there.

Tezozomoc is a Los Angeles Chicano Poet and 2009 Oscar Nominated Activist and has a collection of poetry, "Gashes!: Poems and Pain from the halls of injustice", (Floricanto Press 2019). He has also been published in the following journals: The Oddball Magazine, Spitpoetzine, The Silver Stork. Campanella, Nick. "The 2018 Winter Issue of Come and Go Literary Is Finally Here." The Blue Nib, The Coiled Serpent: Poets Arising from the Cultural Quakes and Shifts of Los Angeles, Men's Heartbreak Anthology, CrazyQuilt, Rhino, Mind Matters Review, Left Curve, Next Phase, Minotaur Press, San Fernando Poetry Journal, Caffeine, and many others.

Joel H. Vega's debut poetry collection 'DRIFT,' won the Philippines 2019 National Book Award for Best Poetry Book in English and was also granted the same honor by the Philippine Literary Arts Council. His poems have appeared in various literary journals in the US, The Philippines, Austria, Germany, France, The Netherlands, and the UK. He lives in Arnhem, The Netherlands, where he works as publications editor.

Edward Vidaurre is an award-winning poet and author of seven collections of poetry. He is the 2018-2019 City of McAllen, Texas Poet Laureate, a five-time Pushcart-nominated poet, and publisher of FlowerSong Press. His writings have appeared in The New York Times, The Texas Observer, Grist, Poet Lore, The Acentos Review, Poetrybay, Voices de la Luna, as well as other journals and anthologies. Vidaurre resides in McAllen, Texas with his wife and daughter.

Stalina Emmanuelle Villarreal lives as a rhyming-slogan creative activist. She is a Generation 1.5 poet (*mexicanx* and Xicanx), a translator, a sonic-improv collaborator, and an instructor of English. She is a Ph.D. candidate in the Creative Writing Program at University of Houston. She coauthored an article with a historian in the book *Chicana Movidas* (University of Texas, 2018). Her poetry can be found in the *Rio Grande Review*, *Texas Review*, *Spoon River Poetry Review*, *The Acentos Review*, *Defunkt Magazine*, and elsewhere. She has published translations of poetry, including *Enigmas*, by Sor Juana Inés de la Cruz (Señal: a project of Libros Antena Books, *BOMB*, and Ugly Duckling Presse, 2015), but she mostly translates *regiomontana* poet Minerva Reynosa; they have a chapbook called *Photograms of My Conceptual Heart, Absolutely Blind* (Cardboard House Press, 2016). She also published *Kilimanjaro* by Maricela Guerrero (Cardboard House Press, 2018).

Sara Whitestone is a novelist-in-progress, an essayist-in-practice, and an un-tortured-poet-in-process. Her words and artwork have appeared in many print and online magazines and journals, and her current long-form project is a novel titled *Wandering*. To learn more about Whitestone's inner and outer adventures, visit sarawhitestone.com and follow her on Instagram and Twitter @sarawhitestone.

Habib Abodunrin Zakari hold a BA Literature in English from Ahmadu Bello University, Zaria. He is a Staff Editor at Second Revolution Literary Magazine and his writings have appeared on Nigerian Newspapers and the quarterly Sentinel Nigeria Magazine. He spends his time teaching, writing, translating books and organizing humanitarian interventions.

EDITORS

Vincent Cooper is the author of Where the Reckless Ones Come to Die and Zarzamora- Poetry of Survival. His poetry has been published with Huizache, Riversedge Journal and Somos En Escrito. He is a member of The Macondo Writers Workshop.

Edward Vidaurre is an award-winning poet and author of seven collections of poetry. He is the 2018-2019 City of McAllen, Texas Poet Laureate, a five-time Pushcart-nominated poet, and publisher of FlowerSong Press. His writings have appeared in The New York Times, The Texas Observer, Grist, Poet Lore, The Acentos Review, Poetrybay, Voices de la Luna, as well as other journals and anthologies. Vidaurre resides in McAllen, Texas with his wife and daughter.